Building & Closing the Sale

Proven Methods for Closing Sales

Virden J. Thornton

A Fifty-Minute™ Series Book

CRISP.
Learning
Menlo Park, California

1-800-442-7477

CrispLearning.com

Building & Closing the Sale

Proven Methods for Closing Sales

Revised Edition of *Closing: A Process, Not a Problem*

Virden J. Thornton

Credits:

Senior Editor: **Debbie Woodbury**
Editor: **Charlotte Bosarge**
Production Manager: **Judy Petry**
Design: **Amy Shayne**
Production Artists: **Darin Stumme, Jake Yeagley**
Cartoonist: **Ralph Mapson**

© 1995, 2001 Crisp Publications, Inc.
Printed in the United States of America by Von Hoffmann Graphics, Inc.

CrispLearning.com

02 03 04 10 9 8 7 6 5 4 3 2

Library of Congress Catalog Card Number 00-106651
Thornton, Virden J.
Building & Closing the Sale: Proven Methods for Closing Sales
ISBN 1-56052-598-3

Learning Objectives For:

BUILDING & CLOSING THE SALE

The objectives for *Building & Closing the Sale* are listed below. They have been developed to guide you, the reader, to the core issues covered in this book.

THE OBJECTIVES OF THIS BOOK ARE:

❑ 1) To increase your chances of consistently successful sales by building rapport and trust

❑ 2) To learn how to address questions and objections with confidence

❑ 3) To show you how to tailor your sales demonstration to each client

❑ 4) To teach you how to ask the right questions and keep your prospect's attention

ASSESSING YOUR PROGRESS

In addition to the learning objectives, Crisp Learning has developed an **assessment** that covers the fundamental information presented in this book. A 25-item, multiple-choice and true-false questionnaire allows the reader to evaluate his or her comprehension of the subject matter. To learn how to obtain a copy of this assessment, please call **1-800-442-7477** and ask to speak with a Customer Service Representative.

Assessments should not be used in any employee selection process.

Preface

I periodically receive books from publishers across the country to review on "selling techniques" and "closing skills." In these books, the authors often list dozens of different closing tools or "tactics," as one writer calls them. Many of these closing methods are extremely high pressure and manipulative. Most of the phrases and questions suggested for closing sales are completely unusable today. Is it surprising then that sales representatives and service industry professionals (accountants, bankers, attorneys, engineers, etc.) fear closing? If high-pressure–and in many cases ethically questionable–closing techniques are all that a professional is taught, it is easy to see why closing a sale can be difficult.

Closing a sale is an ethical process that anyone can learn. The selling process outlined in this self-administered learning guide is designed to alleviate the fear of making presentations and closing sales, and encourages alternative methods to high pressure and manipulation of prospective customers or clients. Once you have mastered the steps described here, you should never have to pressure or manipulate a prospect to buy from you again. Good luck.

Virden J. Thornton

Virden J. Thornton

Dedication

To Marion D. Hanks, a special teacher and leader who changed my life.

To my wife, Barbara, for her love and devotion.

About the Author

As founder, president, and senior advisor at The Selling Edge®, Inc., a training and development firm in Avon Lake, Ohio, Virden J. Thornton has assisted thousands of managers, sales representatives, and service industry professionals (accountants, attorneys, bankers, engineers, etc.) in generating more business for their organizations. A partial client list includes AvFuel; Eastman Kodak; PNC Bank; Jefferson Pilot; National Associates, Inc.; the government of the U.S. Virgin Islands; Service Linen Supply, Inc.; IBM; Bolanis Financial Planning Group, Inc.; City Laundering Co; New York Life; and Wal-Mart. Virden is the author of an acclaimed self-directed learning series of sales, telemarketing, and motivational guides. He is also the author of *Prospecting: The Key to Sales Success* and *Close That Sale,* an audio/videotape program by Crisp Publications. He is a dynamic national speaker and regularly conducts workshops on sales, coaching, and team development, customer service, and motivational topics. Virden and his wife, Barbara, are the parents of 10 children.

Contents

Part 1: Building Rapport

Closing: An Essential Part of the Selling Process 3

Rapport = Trust 8

Pre-Interview Trust Builders 9

Communication Techniques that Build Trust 20

Opportunity: A Favorable Juncture of Circumstances 23

Finding Something in Common Is a Myth 32

Part 2: An Ethical Approach to Closing Success

Uncovering Prospects' Needs 37

Ask a Provocative Question 41

To Obtain the Keys to Fort Knox, Use a Take-Away Transition 44

Avoid the Product or Service Trap 46

Part 3: Ask In-Depth, Probing Questions

Producing Profitable Interactions 51

1. Ask Open-Ended Questions 52

2. Phrase Questions Carefully 54

3. Rephrase and Redirect to Maintain Control 56

4. Deal with Negatives Head-On 58

5. Use the Most Powerful Principle in Communications 61

Part 4: Demonstrations That Close

The Demonstration Phase of Closing 65

Appeal to Your Prospect's Emotions 70

Three Important Rules 71

Give Intellectual Proof 72

Ask Trial Closing Questions 79

Answer Objections as Questions, Not as a Roadblock to Your Sale! 81

Beginning the Close 84

Part 5: Closing Is a Process

Finalizing Your Sale 93

Recognizing Buying Signals 96

Create a Sense of Urgency 98

Just Ask! 100

Summary 102

Additional Reading 103

Building

Rapport

2

Closing: An Essential Part of the Selling Process

The ultimate goal in any selling activity is to tie down the sale. However, closing a sale is difficult for most sales representatives or service industry professionals, often causing many of them to lose sight of this vital objective. For example, one national study on sales communication showed that in over 60% of the sales meetings conducted daily, there is no attempt on the part of the seller to close a sale. Some marketing executives estimate that as many as 50% of all sales representatives and licensed professionals quit after their first sales meeting, and fewer than 12% percent persist until a buyer finally says "yes." As these studies illustrate, you must learn the art of *asking* for business, or your chances of consistently selling your products or services (getting your prospective buyer to take action) will be reduced significantly. Nevertheless, one of the most overrated topics in sales training today is the subject of closing.

The object of most sales courses is to fill the heads of participants with as many closing techniques as possible. More than half of most workshops or seminars will address closing skills. The logic is simple—if the "Ben Franklin" close does not work, the participant is then taught to rummage around in his or her head for the "puppy dog," "secondary question," "order-blank," or "forced choice" close to tie off the sale. ("Forced choice"—now that sounds ethical, doesn't it?)

Today, sales training in many business or professional organizations—if it exists at all—is simply teaching participants about the company's products or services, then drilling them on how to make a "pitch" and memorize a long and complex series of closing techniques. In contrast to this methodology, top sales professionals know that successful selling and closing is part of an overall process and not just the use of hard-sell presentation and closing techniques. They know that if you can learn to show your prospects, customers, or clients that they are better off using your products or services, then the sale is yours.

Closing: An Essential Part of the Selling Process (CONTINUED)

When a sales presentation is made properly, the natural conclusion to the transaction is to close the deal. Most buyers expect to be asked to take action when your sales presentation is followed to its natural conclusion. At this point in a sale, you do not need to use special closing techniques—you simply need to ask for the business.

Closing is actually the easiest part of the selling process. However, most sales representatives and professionals do not believe that closing is easy, because most of today's sales training, as suggested above, teaches the closing process backward. If today's sales training models were diagrammed as a triangle, building relationships with prospective customers or clients would be the little point of the triangle. Teaching prospects about sales presentations products and how to present them would be a broad band in the middle of the illustration, and techniques for closing the sale would be the large base of the triangle.

Using a marriage proposal as an analogy, marketing professional Steven Brown in *American Salesman** suggests that the emphasis on presentation and closing skills puts the sales or service industry professional in the position of a suitor in Victorian England. "He has barely met the girl, but convention demands that he propose marriage before he can get to know her. He uses a well-rehearsed speech to try to persuade her of his worthiness. He has no idea of whether his attention is welcome or utterly inappropriate. He's terrified because everything hinges on her 'Yes' or 'No.'"

An *effective* closing process turns the sales pyramid upside down, with the small point at the bottom. Closing should follow a pattern similar to today's marriage proposal. "Will you marry me?" is most often no more than a rhetorical question, of which both suitors should know the outcome, provided they have a well-established relationship. As Brown suggests, "When he asks for her hand (or when she pops the question), he's pretty sure of getting a 'yes.'" Closing a sales transaction the right way is a natural outcome of a relationship that is built on a foundation of mutual respect and trust.

**Excerpts reprinted with permission of © National Research Bureau, P.O. Box 1, Burlington, Iowa 52601-0001.*

Closing a sale is an integral part of an orchestrated selling process. By first building rapport with your prospect, you create the trust that is vital to closing a sale. No matter how wonderful your product or service is, people will not buy from you unless they trust you! By learning to ask closed-ended, attention-getting questions, you can open your prospect's mind to ultimately accepting your presentation. Open-ended, probing questions can then be asked to learn about needs, hidden feelings, and problems that can be solved by the specific products or services that you represent. By tailoring your demonstration to only those products or services that meet the needs or problems you uncover in your questioning, and by asking trial closing questions, you can determine how your prospect feels about your presentation and the suggested solution to your prospect's problems. Then, by answering any questions or objections your prospect might have, you can set the stage for tying off the transaction. All that is left in the closing process is to simply ask for the business.

Closing: An Essential Part of the Selling Process (CONTINUED)

This self-directed learning tool explores the steps in the selling process that lead to a successful close. You will not be given a dozen closing speeches to memorize. Nor will you receive a long list of power words to compel your prospect to sign on the dotted line. These often questionable tactics simply do not work with today's sophisticated consumers. If you learn and review the steps to closing a sale that are presented here, then apply them in your daily sales activities, you should begin to see a significant difference in your ability to generate business for your organization.

All you need to do is execute the steps or stages of the selling (closing) process properly, and the close will take care of itself. Remember that closing is an integral part of the selling process, not a stand-alone technique. An effective closing process looks something like this:

The Closing Pyramid

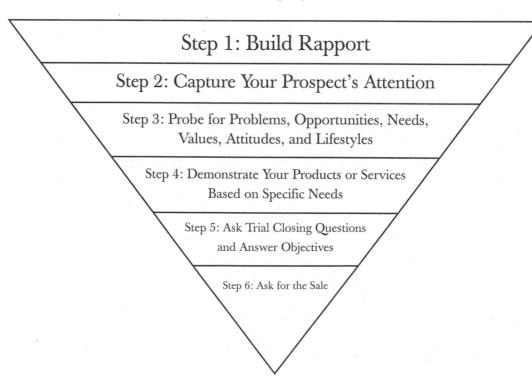

Step 1: Build Rapport

Step 2: Capture Your Prospect's Attention

Step 3: Probe for Problems, Opportunities, Needs, Values, Attitudes, and Lifestyles

Step 4: Demonstrate Your Products or Services Based on Specific Needs

Step 5: Ask Trial Closing Questions and Answer Objectives

Step 6: Ask for the Sale

SELF-ASSESSMENT

Before you go any further, take a few minutes to answer the following questions.

How does your business success compare to projections from a year ago?

_____

_____

_____

Are you meeting your goals? If not, how far off are you?

_____

_____

_____

What specific closing problems do you have?

_____

_____

_____

What do you believe is your biggest barrier to successful closing?

_____

_____

_____

Keep your answers in mind as you read on. This will help you stay focused on getting the most value from this book.

Rapport = Trust

When Joe Gandolfo, a life insurance salesman from a small town in Florida, was asked how he had closed over $1 billion of life insurance in a single year, he said that it was simple—"all it takes is understanding people." Although Joe's response may seem simplistic, his formula can be recommended without hesitation—because it works. In addition, it can work as well for you as it did for Joe Gandolfo or for any other successful sales representative or licensed professional.

In the insurance industry, members get excited about someone who sells in excess of $1 million of life insurance each year. They have an elite group of sales professionals who belong to a Million Dollar Round Table. The Round Table is where individuals are recognized for outstanding sales performance. To put Joe's accomplishment in perspective, it would take an average Million Dollar Round Table producer 1,000 years to equal Joe Gandolfo's one-year production figures.

Joe's level of closing is remarkable. He is one of a distinguished group of sales superstars who has discovered the secret of consistently closing sales. Therefore, when Joe suggests that consistent closings depend on your "ability to understand people," rather than presentation skills, technical ability, or product knowledge, you should pay attention to him. The most important skill in closing is the ability to understand the people you serve and then, through this understanding, build rapport with them. Building rapport is the method top sales and service industry professionals use to develop a feeling of trust in the people they serve. Without trust, buyers will not actively participate in the closing process. Always remember, people buy from a professional whom they trust. So, what do you have to do to build trust? Read and follow the recommendations in this section of the manual.

CLOSING PRINCIPLE **1**

People buy from people they trust.

Pre-Interview Trust Builders

Dress for Success

Looking professional means wearing appropriate attire. If you suspect you might be weak in this area, get a book on the subject of professional dress from your local library. John Molloy's books, *John T. Molloy's New Dress for Success* or *Women's Dress for Success Handbook,* both provide helpful information on appropriate dress for your industry. Although these books are difficult to find, most large metropolitan-area or college libraries have copies in their business sections. In addition, your favorite bookstore may still be able to obtain copies, or you can check online at Barnes & Noble or Amazon.com. John Malloy's recommendations are still valid today because they are based on solid research into how people perceive you, based on the clothes you wear and not simply on how some guru thinks your appearance will affect other people from an aesthetic standpoint.

Remember, little things like facial hair, tattoos, and piercings can reduce your ability to build rapport and close sales by as much as 30%. Ask, "Is a beard or several gold rings or studs really worth the lost revenue?" To judge a book by its cover may not be fair, yet nearly everyone does. Even when people mentally tell themselves not to be hasty in judging others, they still register opinions about another person based on how the individual looks, moves, and dresses. These quick mental judgments are influenced by two important factors—body language and personal appearance. Appearance includes clothing, accessories, hair, skin, makeup, and grooming (cleanliness, body odor, nail care, etc.).

CASE STUDY: FIRST (AND LAST) IMPRESSIONS

If you don't think people base their opinion on how you dress, an article published on the front page of *USA Today* clearly illustrates how susceptible we are to making invalid judgments based on appearance.

John Barrier, dressed in dirty construction clothes, walked into his bank to cash a check for $100. When he presented the check, he also asked that his parking slip be validated to save 60 cents. A bank employee refused to validate the ticket since the customer had not conducted a required deposit transaction. When he informed the employee that he was considered a substantial depositor of the bank, she looked at him as though she did not believe a word he said. He received no better treatment from the manager, who, in Mr. Barrier's words, looked at him as though he had "crawled out from under a rock" because of the way he was dressed. The next day, John Barrier withdrew $1 million from this bank. Who would have believed, based on his appearance, that this man was a multimillionaire?

Your appearance is a power tool that can be used to influence others positively or negatively. As you mentally evaluate people, they are judging you in the same way. How you look, move, and dress influences everyone with whom you interact—your prospects, customers or clients, co-workers, friends, relatives, even strangers. You must recognize the power of the first impression if you expect to consistently close sales.

Psychologists and behaviorists report that when a person dresses more professionally, he acts more professionally as well. You have the ability to create a powerful image of confidence, competence, and professionalism, which in turn will build trust in your potential customers (clients). As a rule, you should always dress one level above your prospect, customer, or client to make a favorable impression and build the kind of trust that leads to closing the sale.

Soften to Build Trust

A study by George Miline and Maria-Eugenia Boaz (Marketing Science Institute Report, 398-117) looked into the relationship between customers who trusted their sales representative and those who did not. This research team concluded that it wasn't a brand name or a firm's corporate image that produced trust in a customer. Trust was formed by the sales representatives themselves:

➤ By the amount and quality of information that the decision-maker received from the representative

➤ By the representative allowing the customer to become part of the selling process

➤ By the number of personal contacts that were made to the prospective buyer

A Stanford University study underscored the Miline and Boaz findings by suggesting that it takes an average of 9 to twelve contacts or impressions before you can effectively close a sale. This research also indicates that the average sales representative or service industry professional quits making impressions after only three contacts. Since finding time to make all of your impressions in person is difficult, you need to find other ways of creating favorable impressions.

Pre-Interview Trust Builders (CONTINUED)

To gain a competitive edge, use the following methods:

➤ Before you contact a decision-maker to set an appointment, send a softening letter to build trust and set the stage for your appointment request.

➤ Be creative in your softening letters. Use headlines and bold-faced type to capture your buyer's attention. Eye-catching headlines and type always give the prospect a reason for reading further.

➤ At The Selling Edge, Inc., we use a small puzzle that is imprinted with our logo and the phrase "Fits All the Pieces Together!" We write a short note on the back of the puzzle about our desire to obtain an appointment, then we place it (broken into pieces) in a small, hand-addressed envelope with a commemorative stamp on the front and send it to the decision-maker to obtain a memorable first impression.

➤ Remember that the sale you are trying to make in the initial stage of trust building is an appointment. Never try to sell your products or services in your softening letter or on the telephone. Just sell the decision-maker on setting up a meeting.

➤ Whenever you obtain a referral, make certain that your prospect knows that a friend or acquaintance has recommended you.

➤ Always give the decision-maker a reason for making an appointment with you.

➤ Use an odd-sized envelope, not your corporate stationary envelope, hand-address it, and use a commemorative stamp to get past the "gatekeepers" that will screen you out.

An effective softening letter might look something like this:

Mr. Gary Buyer
Sr. Vice President
P.D.Q. Industries
123 Any Street
Anytown, USA 99999

Dear Gary:

Saving Money on Replacement Kits

Jerry Jones suggested that I contact you. If you felt you could save over 25% on the cost of a 269A replacement kit and, in the process, significantly improve delivery times and after-sale service, would you give me 15, no more than 20, minutes to explain our new pricing structure?

I'll be in Anytown on Wednesday the 15th and then back again the following Thursday the 23rd. I'll call in a day or two to see which of these two days would be best for a short meeting.

Sincerely,

Roberta Seller
Regional Manager

P.S. The XYZ Company is now experiencing a 35% reduction in replacement time using our new 269A kits.

Pre-Interview Trust Builders (CONTINUED)

Let's review the individual parts of this letter to see why it is an effective rapport-builder and good softening tool.

➤ The letter visually catches a prospect's attention and subliminally says the sender is creative. At The Selling Edge, we pin a button with the "no problem" logo onto the letter.

➤ By using the button, we get over a 50% higher readership from the softening letters we send.

➤ By mentioning the referral, the letter builds rapport with the prospective buyer.

➤ Most people buy from their emotions, so using the words "If you felt…" helps the reader focus on his feelings about the benefits that follow. In addition, the words "If you felt…" set up a hypothetical question, so there is less pressure being applied than if you asked, "How do you feel about…."

➤ The first part of the letter gives the reader a reason for reading further. It appeals to the number-one buying motive—greed (making money or saving money).

➤ By including three more benefits after the price reduction (reduced delivery time, increased service, and—later in the P.S.—a reduction in replacement time), the sender has a good chance of at least hitting a prospect's hot button so he or she will consider making an appointment.

➤ Although specific benefits of the sender's replacement kits are mentioned, the letter only tries to soften the prospect for an appointment and does not try to sell the product.

➤ This letter gives the specific time needed for an appointment. Most busy executives can spare 15 to 20 minutes. Top sales representatives know that attention spans dictate very short initial contacts. If, at the time, you cannot give a presentation in 15 to 20 minutes, the ideas in this learning guide should help you shorten your sales presentation.

➤ The letter gives an either/or option on the dates the representative is available, which helps a decision-maker in setting an appointment.

➤ Use the P.S. to make an important point. Research shows that people usually read the headline and the P.S. of a letter. If you have endorsement letters, find a way to place an endorsement in the P.S. of your softening letter.

A softening letter should help you increase the number of appointments you make. If constructed properly, it can also turn cold calling into a much warmer process.

Practice

Take a few minutes now to construct your own softening letter. Use the sample and the comments above to assist you in creating a favorable impression.

_____

_____

_____

_____

_____

_____

_____

_____

_____

_____

_____

_____

You need to be creative in finding ways to make a favorable impression with a prospective buyer before your initial contact. On the next page is an example of the type of pre-call creativity (sales promotion) that can help you close more sales.

CASE STUDY: A CREATIVE APPROACH

Some years ago, a young sales representative was having a difficult time obtaining appointments with the presidents of firms that could use his products. After being screened continually by assistants and secretaries, he decided to try another approach. First, he purchased some small cardboard boxes with lids that would close tightly. He then punched a series of small holes in the ends of each container. With his thumb, he poked a much larger hole from the inside out through one end of the box, leaving a jagged opening where he had punched his holes. In each box, he placed straw until the box was about half full. On top of the straw he inserted a small feather before sealing the container. Finally, he attached to each of the boxes a card personally addressed to the president of the firms he wanted to visit. He then personally delivered the boxes to each executive's office. Before the representative could return to his office from making his deliveries, his phone started ringing with appointments from the same secretaries who earlier had screened him out. The note on the card was the reason he received a 100% response from the busy executives. It read:

CONTINUED

Mr. Bill McCann
The McCann Agency
1234 Madison Avenue
Lakewood, OH 44034

Dear Bill:

I have been trying to get through to you for some time now to tell you about a product that could save your firm a large amount of money over the next few years. I only need about 30 minutes of your time to demonstrate my product. I thought if I sent you this box as a gift, there was a good chance it would be given to you and then you would see this message. To make it easy to reply, I have placed a homing pigeon in the box. Just put your answer about an appointment on a small piece of paper and slip it in the tube on the leg of the pigeon, then let it go. I'll do the rest.

Sincerely,

Bob Miller

P.S. I could only afford young birds and they are a bit more active than I had planned. If by chance the bird gets out of the box, you can still contact me at 1-800-555-5430.

The Time Factor—Being Punctual Builds Trust

Some professionals feel that being on time for meetings or sales appointments means being no more than 15 minutes late. It seems that being prompt is just not important to some people in this new millennium. Being on time is not an old-fashioned or antiquated concept, no matter how many people fail to understand its impact on trust. The negative impression that being late leaves on others can be seen and felt at the onset of a sales or follow-through meeting. A late arrival begins your relationship with most decision-makers on a negative note.

You have heard someone say, "If he says he'll be here, he'll be on time." These words convey a feeling of trust on the part of the speaker, for the individual who is yet to arrive. This person is well known for his promptness and, in turn, is trusted and respected for this trait. Although a seemingly mundane issue to many sales and service industry professionals, being on time is vital to building the trust needed to consistently close prospects, customers, or clients.

Benefits to Being on Time:

➤ You have the time to relax and get into a friendly state of mind, so you do not appear harried and stressed.

➤ It is a sign of respect for your prospective customers or clients.

➤ You have time to learn more about the company and your prospect. This information may be just what you need to build rapport with your prospective buyer.

When you are on time, it demonstrates to your buyer that you are a professional who can be trusted.

CLOSING PRINCIPLE 2

People make buying decisions based on their first impressions.

PUNCTUALITY REVIEW

Place a check (✔) in the box that best describes your use of time.

	Always	Usually	Rarely
1. I am on time for my business appointments.	❏	❏	❏
2. I am on time for my personal appointments.	❏	❏	❏
3. Punctuality is a trait I value in others and myself.	❏	❏	❏
4. I do a good job of arranging my schedule and giving myself enough time to accomplish my tasks.	❏	❏	❏
5. I know how to prioritize my time.	❏	❏	❏
6. I include room in my schedule for unexpected events.	❏	❏	❏
7. I prepare a daily list of "to do" tasks to help keep me focused.	❏	❏	❏
8. I consult my daily calendar.	❏	❏	❏
9. I do an analysis of my time use at least once a year to ensure that I am making the best use of my time.	❏	❏	❏
10. I feel in control of my time.	❏	❏	❏

Review all items you marked "Rarely." You might find that by getting control of each of these low-rated items, you will have better control of your time and be more punctual for your appointments.

Communication Techniques That Build Trust

Research conducted by Motivational Systems of West Orange, New Jersey, found that 72% of 12,000 participants reported that in first-time meetings, nonverbal communication carried significantly more weight than a person's verbal communication. This study revealed that only 6% of the survey respondents paid the slightest attention to what a person was saying at a first-time meeting.

Similar conclusions from research conducted by Dr. Al Mehrabian at UCLA found that only 7% of a person's communications effectiveness comes from words, while 38% is made up of a person's tone of voice and 55% from nonverbal forms of communication such as eye contact, gestures, body language, dress, etc. That means 93% of what is effectively communicated is nonverbal. It seems that your body language and tone of voice speak more loudly than actual words.

Remember, trying to talk a decision-maker into having a great first impression of you is impossible, no matter how hard you may try. In order to make great first impressions, you need to become aware of what your body language and appearance are saying and then take control over these nonverbal messages. This is especially true of a first-time meeting. At your first meeting, just relax, have confidence in your ability, and let the buyer size you up from your "nonverbal communication."

Body language reflects your prospect's true feelings, just as it does your own. By carefully observing those to whom you sell, you can pick up on negative nonverbal signals early in the transaction. Through close observation, you should be able to spot when your buyer is visually telling you that she is uncertain, needs more information, wants an opportunity to ask questions, or is strongly opposed to your suggestions.

Practice

What type of nonverbal signs have you noticed from your prospects?

_____

_____

_____

The value of understanding nonverbal communication becomes more apparent when you realize that for most people, the messages "given off" unconsciously are more valid indicators of a buyer's true feelings than his words. Most prospects will ultimately make a decision to buy from you based on their feelings. You can get in touch with how a person feels by simply observing his or her gestures, posture, tilt of head, etc.

MASTERING NONVERBAL COMMUNICATION

Place a check (✔)in each box that reflects your understanding of the importance of body language and nonverbal communication.

❏ I have read at least one article or book on the importance and value of understanding body language.

❏ I have good listening skills.

❏ I am an effective persuader.

❏ I am aware of the different styles of communication of my co-workers and clients.

❏ I look for ways to learn and apply new communication strategies.

❏ Self-understanding is a real key to effective interpersonal communication.

❏ I pay attention to where I look when I talk to my clients.

❏ I have worked with a friend or co-worker to identify and eliminate my nervous gestures.

❏ I know the importance of putting a smile in my voice.

❏ My body-language skills convey credibility and believability with my clients.

Each item above should have a check next to it. For any unchecked item, plan to review it on a regular basis until you can confidently place a check by it.

———————

For a useful book on this subject, consider ordering The Art of Communicating *by Bert Decker, Crisp Publications.*

Opportunity: A Favorable Juncture of Circumstances

In the studies by Dr. Mehrabian mentioned earlier, he found that people make decisions whether to follow your advice and eventually buy from you in the *first two minutes* of your conversation. By following the techniques outlined below, you can make the most of your initial contact and truly turn each outside sales call or inside transaction into a favorable juncture of circumstances (a closing opportunity).

Shake your prospect's hand and smile warmly

A warm, firm, friendly handshake goes a long way in building a trusting relationship. It sends a message without words:

➤ Professionalism

➤ Personal touch

➤ Self-confidence

➤ Warmth

➤ Genuineness

It tells your buyer that you are a friendly person and that you are glad to see him. If a person shakes your hand as if it were a wet dishrag or a steel bar, it sends other messages, doesn't it? Therefore, you must develop a confident, firm handshake (not an overbearing viselike grip or a limp, wishy-washy grasp). Remember, you only have one chance to make a great first impression.

Opportunity: A Favorable Juncture of Circumstances (CONTINUED)

Let your smile be a warm, sincere expression of the positive feelings you have about meeting someone new, or an old acquaintance. No matter what kind of day you are having, a smile will give those you contact a feeling of acceptance. It will also help you feel better about your day. Top sales professionals use the technique of thinking of a funny story or the latest joke they have heard just before meeting a decision-maker. Also, make sure you are smiling as you telephone for appointments or conduct telephone interviews. You can hear a smile in a person's voice on the telephone, so put a large yellow "smiley face" or the word "SMILE" on your telephone to remind you to regularly use this effective communications tool.

Practice

List three ways that you can use to bring your positive attitude back into focus:

1. _____

2. _____

3. _____

Use First Names

The next step in the rapport-building process is to simply introduce yourself, get on a first-name basis as quickly as possible, and then use your decision-maker's first name throughout your interview or presentation. Prospective customers or clients like the personal attention when you use their name throughout a sales presentation. Successful professionals understand that remembering and using names can often mean the difference between closing success and closing failure.

When you are introduced to a person, you begin to forget the name you heard in less than three seconds. Writing down a person's name in your day planner, in an organizer, or on a pad is a good habit to develop. When a name is written in front of you, you have it to use repeatedly during your conversation with a decision-maker, or later when you are calling back to follow through on your presentation.

Calling people by their first name puts you on an equal footing. When you are in doubt about using someone's first name, just ask: "May I call you…?" The only exception to the rule for getting on a first-name basis is for prospects with titles, such as Dr., Rev., etc. Using their title shows respect, and these professionals will respond favorably when you use their hard-earned titles.

How can you learn to remember names? First, really listen to the name when you are introduced. Really, listen! Ask the person to repeat it if you are not sure you heard the correct pronunciation. Most people are flattered that you care enough to want to get their names right. Another way is to try to "link" their name with something familiar, something already in your mind. Also, repeat the name several times, as you work with your prospect. Repeating the name will help implant it in your mind.

Develop your own mental techniques for remembering names when they are spoken to you. One of the most well-known methods is to use mental pegs or hooks through the use of word associations. When you hear a name, draw a mental picture of it.

Example: "Bob Harrington"

Visualization: Picture a herring bobbing in the waves.

Why to go all this trouble? When you regularly use people's names, you make them feel important. It sends a message that the person means enough to you for you to remember his name. When you make people feel important, they respect your professionalism and begin to like you as a person and trust you as a friend.

Ask Open-Ended Personal Questions

Try using the Who, What, Where, When, Why, and How method of questioning. "Open-ended" questions that begin with these words require an explanation rather than a "yes" or "no" response. Another way to encourage a lengthier response is to say, "Tell me about.…" When decision-makers talk about themselves, psychologists suggest that they begin to build a trusting relationship with you.

In an effective sales interview, your prospect should do 60% to 70% of the talking. This means that you must listen 60% to 70% of the time.

Opportunity: A Favorable Juncture of Circumstances (CONTINUED)

Become a proficient questioner and an interested listener by practicing. When someone is talking, whether it is a co-worker, friend, or family member, listen first, then ask a question that will get the speaker to continue. Listen again and ask another question. Questions should arise naturally from what you hear.

> *"When did this happen?"*
>
> *"Why did that happen?"*
>
> *"Where were you when it happened?"*
>
> *"How did you feel when it happened?"*
>
> *"What would prevent it from happening again?"*

Find something about the other person you can honestly admire and then try to ask an open-ended question based on the prospective client's response:

Sales or Service Professional:	*Your ring intrigues me. Is it an antique?*
Prospect, Client, or Customer:	*It looks like one—that's why I like it. Actually I purchased it on the Internet.*
Sales or Service Professional:	*I have never had good luck with buying things on the Web. How do you know which companies are reliable?*

You cannot pre-plan every question you will ask when you are building rapport. Developing good questions takes practice but, more importantly, it takes a genuine interest in other people. If you are curious about people, the "right" questions will come naturally in your conversation.

Always remember to concentrate on what your prospect is saying. Sometimes you are so concerned about what you will say next or what question you'll ask next that you can miss real opportunities with decision-makers, because you are not really listening to them.

Never use trick questions or traps that are sometimes taught in books on selling or in workshops, just to induce a prospect to agree with you. This type of questioning will often kill a sale.

Right-Eye Contact Builds Trust

Psychologists tell us that a great way to build rapport is to look in the dominant eye of someone who is speaking. Since figuring out if a person is left- or right-brain dominant can be a hassle, and because the vast majority of your prospects are right-eye dominant, just use the right eye (left-brain dominant) contact.

Right-eye contact is based on a principle called "psychological reciprocity." Reciprocity means to give a person something back when you have received a favor, and it is a powerful sales and closing tool. This law is so ingrained in us that we regularly keep ledgers in our head (like owing someone a lunch) to make certain that we are not found breaking the rules. If we forget, we might get the reputation of being a "deadbeat" or worse.

In our culture, psychologists have found there is a quantum effect to reciprocity. Often a small gift or favor will produce a much larger return. Easter seals are a good example of how this quantum effect works. For a small packet of seals, the charity receives donations many times over the cost of the stamps.

When you look a prospective customer or client in her right (or dominant) eye while she is speaking, you are giving her something she seldom receives from other people. Rarely can she get this from her boss, spouse, children, or even other sales professionals. Therefore, by the rules of reciprocity, she is impelled to give you something in return. When you give your complete attention by looking into a buyer's dominant eye, you are saying that she is an important person. Not only does this build trust, but also, in return, your prospect will be attentive to you when you are speaking. Right-eye contact is so powerful that it can also help you close the sale.

Opportunity: A Favorable Juncture of Circumstances (CONTINUED)

Be Other-Centered

Sometimes sales or service industry professionals become so anxious to get people to like them that they inadvertently become focused on themselves rather than on their prospects. It happens so subtly that you can be in the middle of a conversation and suddenly realize you have forgotten your prospect's name, even though you introduced yourself just moments before. Unfortunately, most people can always sense if you are tuned in to them. You should not proceed with the closing process until you are totally focused on the other person.

By focusing on the other person, you indirectly say to the individual, "You are the most important person in this office at this time." Besides extending a compliment and asking questions, here are two more techniques you can use to help your decision-maker feel you are focusing attention on him.

1. In addition to focusing on your buyer's right eye when she is speaking, try to carefully imitate her mood and manner. Do not be obvious, but if your prospect is abrupt, you need to be quick and concise. If the prospect is relaxed, you need to be relaxed as well. Move quickly into your decision-maker's physiology (i.e., imitate the cadence in her speech, her tone of voice, and her body language). Then after a period of replicating her physiology, slowly move into your own sales physiology as you ask in-depth probing questions and make your presentation.

2. Moving into a selling physiology is a process of sitting tall on the edge of your chair with both feet planted firmly under you. Your hands should be free to demonstrate key points using a note pad, product book, flip chart, or sales literature. As you move slowly from your prospect's physiology into a selling position, you also need to move your chair closer to her desk, and into "her space." If she moves toward you as you move forward, you know that your decision-maker is interested in what you are discussing. If she backs away as you move toward her desk, you know that you must build more rapport before initiating your presentation.

CLOSING PRINCIPLE **3**

People buy from people like themselves.

These techniques can help you to better understand your prospect's feelings. A good sales communicator is keenly aware of the mood of the decision-maker being sold.

Note: Some people don't like to talk about their personal lives or interests. They are more concerned about getting results, being efficient, and not wasting time. A sales or service industry professional should be alert to those these feelings and messages and should respond appropriately. You can still build rapport and trust with a "results-oriented individual"—simply focus on what is important to him. Act efficient, businesslike, and professional. To get this kind of person talking, ask issue- or business-related questions. Do not try to "chitchat" or make idle conversation.

As suggested earlier, the first few moments of interaction with people are the most important to the rapport-building process and, ultimately, the closing process as well. When people meet you, their mental computers analyze everything about you to see if you are someone they can like and trust. You get only one chance to make a great first impression. However, when you succeed, you set the stage for a long-term professional relationship and a successful close to your presentation or transaction.

Another powerful "other-centered" technique for building instant rapport with prospective customers or clients is to first obtain a referral, then ask the person making the recommendation to tell you something your source likes or admires about the person being referred. Follow this script:

Ask your referral source, "Tell me, Charlie, is there something you admire about Walt or something I could use to open up our conversation?"

Next, tell your prospect, "Charlie Swank suggested that I call you about _____. Chuck is a real fan of yours. He told me...."

Then tell your prospect the positive things that you discussed with the source of your referral.

Opportunity: A Favorable Juncture of Circumstances (CONTINUED)

Ask Light, Probing Questions

Light probing means that before you get into in-depth fact finding, you need to ask a series of open-ended questions to keep your prospect talking. Talking not only strengthens the rapport that you are building with your prospect, but also sets the stage for the second phase in the closing process—capturing your prospect's attention. At this point in the selling (closing) process, just ask enough open-ended questions to keep your prospect talking and focused on himself and his situation. Also, ask your prospective customer or client a few closed-ended questions that require a "yes." Answering "yes" at this point in the process helps your prospect establish a positive frame of mind.

RAPPORT BUILDING CHECKUP

Rate yourself on a scale of 1 to 5, with 1 being an area that you don't know how well you really are doing; 3 being an area that needs work, and 5 being an area that you feel you have mastered. Circle the appropriate number for each statement.

1 = Don't know 3 = Needs work 5 = Mastered	

1. I regularly mirror my prospects to make them feel more at ease.	1　2　3　4　5
2. I am punctual for my appointments.	1　2　3　4　5
3. I have good listening skills and use them to find opportunities to engage my prospects in conversation.	1　2　3　4　5
4. My handshake is firm, not weak and limp, and not viselike, either.	1　2　3　4　5
5. My wardrobe is well thought-out and professional looking.	1　2　3　4　5
6. I avoid making snap judgments about my clients' decision-makers as much as possible.	1　2　3　4　5
7. I use lots of Who, What, Why, etc., kinds of questions with my prospects.	1　2　3　4　5
8. I know how to make someone feel comfortable.	1　2　3　4　5
9. In the past year I have used at least one prospecting technique that others felt was especially creative.	1　2　3　4　5
10. I put a smile in my voice when I talk to my prospects.	1　2　3　4　5

Don't be surprised or discouraged if you have more 1s or 2s than you have 4s or 5s. There are many elements needed to consistently build rapport, and you often overlook several important ones as you concentrate on what is familiar to you. Review the sections containing information on those methods where you were weak and, if necessary, find a colleague or friend and do role-play exercises to sharpen your skills and awareness.

Finding Something in Common Is a Myth

Finding something in common with a prospective customer or client is nice, but the chances of doing so are extremely low in today's diverse society. For years, sales trainers have taught that small talk and finding common ground is a prerequisite for building rapport. If "finding common ground" happens naturally in the course of your presentation—that's great. However, rather than trying to find common ground in the first few minutes of an interview, it is far better to ask an open-ended personal question to get your prospect talking about herself. Some decision-makers will prefer to get down to business with as little chitchat as possible, but most will need a warm-up period before you proceed with the next step in the closing process.

CASE STUDY: DON'T ATTEMPT TO FAKE IT

A young sales representative tried to fake a conversation about golf with a prospect, only to learn later in the discussion that the executive detested the sport. The sales rep had chosen the subject because near the prospect's coat tree in a corner of his office stood a beautiful set of new golf clubs. It turned out that the clubs were to be given away as a prize as part of the firm's sponsorship of a Ladies Professional Golf Association (LPGA) tournament. The decision-maker hated every minute of his assignment to work with the tournament. In trying to find something in common, the representative brought out all of his prospect's negative feelings about his involvement in the tournament. Not surprisingly, the sales associate did not fare well in closing this executive on his firm's offered services.

ICEBREAKERS AND SMALL TALK

Think back to your last appointments that produced less-than-expected results. Reflect a moment on your choice of small talk and icebreakers. Did you try to find elements in common with your prospect? Did you try to bring something personal into the conversation?

How do you usually break down the communication barriers with new prospects?

_____

_____

Do you find that you use the same openings or introductions on everyone?

_____

_____

How do you pull the prospects' surroundings (trophies, plaques, unusual artwork, photographs, etc.) into your small talk?

_____

_____

If these were not very successful, what else do you remember from their surroundings that you might be able to bring into your opening small talk?

_____

_____

List some questions that you will try on your next appointment:

_____

_____

34

P A R T 2

An Ethical
Approach to
Closing Success

Uncovering Prospects' Needs

You will notice that until now in the rapport-building phase of the closing process, neither you nor your prospect has mentioned any products or services. As you begin the selling, you may be tempted to tell your prospect everything you can about your organization and its products or services. However, successful sales and service professionals know that enticing prospects to talk about themselves, their problems, and their needs is more effective than giving any pitch or presentation. There will be time enough for you to sell your products or services after you have created a climate of trust and friendship with a buyer.

Some people say that they build rapport with their prospect after they have conducted their demonstration, once the prospect has been shown what they can do and the transaction is complete. While it is true that rapport is something you build throughout a presentation, your closing results can be much higher if time is spent building rapport up front—within the first few minutes (one to three minutes) of your conversation, when first impressions give you the benefit of the doubt. Remember that people buy from people they trust. If you wait until after your presentation to create trust, you have little trust on which to close the sale or build an ongoing relationship.

Uncovering Prospects' Needs (CONTINUED)

Once your light probing begins to wane, as it will naturally, you can then ask your prospect about her present situation. At this point, you need to listen closely to what she tells you, because most of the time she will give you clues about what she really needs—not the specific products or services she needs, but the personal concerns, problems, and needs she has. For example, if the prospect says, "I'm interested in reducing my costs," you should be able to determine the prospect's unspoken needs or motivation. If she feels she is paying too much for her present products or services, she is probably not pleased with the service or quality she is receiving either. But, more importantly, you know:

➤ She is looking for a new professional relationship or product line.

➤ She has been spending money on products or services that are similar to yours.

➤ She will listen to your presentation.

When you identify your decision-maker's primary need, you will begin to know exactly how to interest her in your products or services.

What if your prospect says, "I want to learn more about your products or services" but does not give you any more clues? Then you need to put on your detective's hat and dig for more information, using some of the techniques listed in this training guide. You should always want to know why the prospective customer or client gave you an appointment or came in to your office, store, or shop. When you know why, you will also know your prospect's primary need. Once you know her need, you will know how to interest her in your merchandise or services. Remember: Do not fall into the trap of discussing your products or services before uncovering your prospect's needs. If you discuss your wares before you complete the necessary first steps, you could fall into a trap that will be difficult to overcome.

Uncovering Hidden Motivations

As you work with each prospective customer or client, you need to take note of all the clues he gives you about the kind of person he is and what motivates his buying decisions. Sometimes the clues are obscure, and you have to read between the lines and then clarify by asking additional questions. For example, if your prospect says, "I've heard about your special small-business services. My office is close by, so I thought I'd drop in," you might clarify the clues this way:

Seller: *"Who is providing these services for you at the present time, Bill?"*

Prospect: *"I have been working with Stevens & Company way over on Main Street."*

Seller: *"How do you feel about the services you are receiving from Stevens?"*

Prospect: *"Well, that's the reason I'm here. I think the people at Stevens believe our company is too small for them. Over the last few months, the service I have been getting has not lived up to their promises."*

Seller: *"What has troubled you most about their service level?"*

Prospect: *"We estimate time and costs with the reports they provide, and when they're late it is a real problem staying on top of things."*

At this point, you know several things about this individual:

➤ Convenience is not his primary need, but it bears some consideration in his mind.

➤ He is unhappy with his current relationship and he is shopping for a new package of services.

➤ His business is small and he uses an outside vendor in place of staff to provide some vital services.

What is this prospect's most important need? It is receiving personal attention. Although this need is unspoken, a good detective should be able to identify it.

Uncovering Prospects' Needs (CONTINUED)

When you know what motivates a prospect to make decisions, you also know how to sell to that person. This is not manipulation, it is an ethical way to help your buyer get what she really wants and needs.

Researchers consolidate people's needs into one or more of the following categories:

➤ Personal attention

➤ Convenience or ease

➤ Saving or making money

➤ Safety

When you are able to satisfy a decision-maker's hidden needs, you turn a prospect into a satisfied customer or client. In addition, the customer or client you have acquired will remain loyal as long as you stay aware of his needs. The following techniques can help you set the stage for in-depth probing to uncover hidden needs as well as those problems and opportunities that are obvious to you and your prospect.

CLOSING PRINCIPLE 4

Most people buy from their emotions.

Ask a Provocative Question

Once you have discovered a bit more about your buyer and her organization by asking a series of light probing questions, you are then ready to ask a provocative question. A provocative question is a powerful communication tool that can open the mind of your decision-maker. Created originally by the consultants at David Yoho and Associates in Fairfax, Virginia, it was designed to help telemarketers open the minds of prospective buyers on the telephone. However, the technique was such a valuable method for capturing a prospect's attention that it was tested by The Selling Edge, Inc., staff. In face-to-face selling situations, it was found to be even more effective with decision-makers. A provocative question is a query that provokes interest. It is a carefully phrased question designed to capture your prospect's attention and make her think. For example:

"Susan, if you felt you could save money and cut your error rate in half by having a firm like ours handle your program, would you consider purchasing our services today?"

A well-executed provocative question turns on a switch in your prospect's mind. It opens your a decision-maker's subconscious to the sale of your products or services. It has an easy-to-follow formula that rarely fails. You construct a provocative question like this:

If you felt **you could** (benefit), (benefit), **and** (benefit),

would you (action desired)?

The words "if you felt" are used for a specific reason. They help a buyer to think about how the benefits you have presented would make her feel. Remember, most prospects buy from their emotions or feelings, and then they justify the decision they have made with their intellect. When selling, you must create a certain amount of tension in your discussion to bring about a favorable decision from a buyer. The words "If you felt..." set up a hypothetical situation that builds just the right amount of tension to persuade a decision-maker to think positively about your offer, but is rarely viewed by a prospect as a hard-sell tactic.

When you add benefits to the words "If you felt..." make certain that they are important to your prospect. We call these "you benefits." They answer your prospect's question: "What's in it for me?"

To avoid overwhelming a decision-maker with too many concepts, use one or two (but no more than three) personal benefits after each "If you felt…" question.

Usually, these benefits will come from your conversation with and light probing of a decision-maker, as you built rapport in the beginning stages of your promotion. If you think a prospect's primary need is better service, then stress that in your provocative question. If the secondary need is cost containment, try this kind of provocative question:

                               benefit 1   **benefit 2**

If you felt **you could** improve your service levels at a retainer rate lower

                                      action

than you pay now, **would you** consider hiring our firm?

The end of a provocative question should indicate the action you want your prospect to take:

> *"…would you make a purchase decision today?"*

> *"…would you make an appointment for a full presentation?"*

> *"…would you switch vendors?"*

> *"…would you purchase the discounted model?"*

USING PROVOCATIVE QUESTIONS

Accountants, attorneys, engineers, architects, bankers, and sales professionals who are "rainmakers" for their firms or businesses become skilled at using the provocative question simply through repeated practice of the technique. To help you practice, write a provocative question for each of the following prospects.

1. Sarah Barnett is senior vice president for a medium-sized manufacturing firm. She wants quality service at the best possible prices. Her hidden need is that she would like to change services from her current vendor, but is afraid to make the decision (she recently was promoted to this new position).

   _____

   _____

   _____

2. Tom Jackson travels a great deal in his position. He does not like waiting and wants to be able to discuss his concerns through email and over the telephone. He also wants to schedule time for reviewing his needs during those limited days when he is not on the road.

   _____

   _____

   _____

Now review what you have learned to this point. First, you build rapport by asking questions, using the decision-maker's name and focusing all of your attention on her. Then you try to identify her key issues or needs. Next, you lightly probe for the prospect's hidden needs. Then you work to capture her attention by asking a provocative question that asks how she feels about the benefits you can provide her company or firm.

To Obtain the Keys to Fort Knox, Use a Take-Away Transition

As you read the title above, you are probably scratching your head and wondering: "After I went to all the trouble to capture the decision-maker's attention, why would I want to take it all away?" To discover why, let's analyze human behavior.

Psychologically, think how you are affected when you want something and someone says, "You can't have it." Most of us want the thing even more. A successful sales or service industry professional should:

1. Uncover a prospective client or customer's need.

2. Arouse the prospect's interest about how the need can be met.

3. Say, "I'm not certain what I have in mind is right for your division."

A take-away transition follows a provocative question like this:

Provocative Question: *"Jim, if you felt you could obtain a higher level of service with timely reporting and reduce the time your staff spends in this area of your business, would you be interested in obtaining our small-business-services package?"*

Prospect: *"Yes, that sounds like what I need."*

Take-away transition: *"Well, I'm not certain if what I have in mind will work for you. Tell me more about your present situation so I can determine if our services will work."*

We call this a take-away transition, because the take-away helps you move from the rapport-building phase in the selling process to the in-depth probing phase. This take-away also helps you obtain permission from the prospect to ask all the questions that are traditionally difficult to ask, such as "What problems have you experienced with your present vendor?" "How much money are you presently spending on your _____ service now?" "You and who else will be making the final decision to change _____ services?" "What obstacles do you see in getting started now?" "What is the best payment structure for your firm?"

When a selling professional asks, "Let me ask you a few questions"—telegraphing her intentions to probe for information—the average buyer automatically resists offering additional insight into his situation, even if he is interested or needs what the sales representative is selling. By using a well-thought-out Provocative Question/Take-away Transition, you can effectively eliminate or reduce this built-in resistance to your in-depth probing questions and even create a desire in your prospect to volunteer information. Think about it. When you enter a store and you know exactly what you want to purchase, as the salesclerk approaches, what do you automatically say? That's right…"I'm just looking, thank you." Even though you could use the salesperson's help, since we are all programmed to resist a selling situation, you initially avoid working with the clerk. The take-away transition helps you to ask questions—even pointed questions—without causing a decision-maker to resist you.

There are no specific words to memorize with a take-away. The exact words you select are not as important as the psychological message that you send. You simply plant a seed of doubt in the prospect's mind that perhaps she might not qualify for the series of benefits you have suggested.

Avoid the Product or Service Trap

Sometimes when you use a provocative question to capture your prospect's attention, your prospect will focus on a specific product or service that you mention.

Seller: *"George, if you felt you could increase the level of service you receive and also reduce the fees your dealership spends on your basic services by purchasing our small-business package, would you switch vendors?"*

George: *"Do you mean I could get a better price from your firm for the same services?"*

If you directly answer the prospect's question, you could inadvertently fall into a real trap. Watch:

Seller: *"Yes. For as little as $1,250 per month, we could provide you with the five basic services you now receive from XYZ & Associates, Inc."*

George: *"$1,250 doesn't come close to XYZ's incentive package. Are you sure you want to do business with our dealership?"*

Do you recognize the trap? It's called the product or service trap. Once you get caught up in discussing any product or service before you fully know a prospect's needs and situation, you significantly reduce your chances of closing a sale. An important rule to embed in your subconscious mind is: Discuss your services only after you have uncovered all of a potential customer's or client's needs and you know her exact situation. In the closing process outlined here, discussion of your products or services does not begin until you have completed the in-depth probing phase of the process.

When a prospect focuses on one aspect of your provocative question, return to your system and use the take-away transition.

Seller: *"I'll be glad to explain how our small-business package works, George, but I'm not sure if it will work for your dealership. I need to get some more information about your present situation."*

Remain in Control

Using the provocative question and take-away transition together provides you with a strong technique for maintaining control of your presentation. When a prospective client or customer takes control of the discussion (by asking questions), he will often draw you into talking about specific services. Moreover, a product-driven presentation has much less chance of succeeding than the closing system outlined here in this guide. Remember, the person who asks the questions in a sales transaction controls the discussion.

Let's look at our example with George. He seemed interested in improving his service levels and reducing his fee for some basic services. However, the service professional really needed to know where George was coming from before discussing the features and benefits of her service package. You will not have a good idea of a prospect's needs and specific situation until you have an opportunity to ask him a number of questions during the probing portion of your interview—which is set up by using a take-away transition.

One other point to remember about a provocative question is that you still have a chance to successfully close even if the prospect says, "No, that's not what I want." When this happens, the prospect is simply saying, "You have misread my real needs, try again." This is how it works:

Seller: *"So, Joan, if you felt you could conveniently transfer information to us by telephone without having to come to our office, would that interest you?"*

Joan: *"No, I don't think so."*

Seller: *"I'm sorry, I must have misunderstood. I thought that convenience was a real concern for you because of your hectic travel schedule."*

Joan: *"Well, it is important, but if I don't handle the transactions personally, I feel that something may go wrong. Anyway, I really don't trust the telephone lines for this vital information."*

Now the sales representative should ask another provocative question that refocuses on Joan's expressed needs. If Joan says, "yes" this time, then the seller should follow up with a take-away transition.

REMAINING IN CONTROL

Take a few minutes now to write another provocative question that refocuses on Joan's needs, and then write a take-away transition to go with your provocative question:

Provocative Question:

_____

_____

_____

_____

_____

_____

_____

_____

Take-away Transition:

_____

_____

_____

_____

_____

_____

_____

_____

_____

Ask In-Depth, Probing Questions

Producing Profitable Interactions

In-depth probing (or the interview phase) of the closing process will help you identify your buyer's needs and wants. Probing can also provide you with information you need to build an ongoing business relationship. This step helps you uncover additional needs that perhaps even your prospect is not consciously aware she may have.

Probing for opportunities helps a sales or service professional close without pressure. As you ask questions, you will find your prospect telling you her concerns, likes, dislikes, etc. She will give you clues about what her objections might be. Then you can neutralize the objections in a comfortable, nonthreatening way, long before her objections become a major block to closing the sale. In addition, the in-depth probing phase of the process helps you to strengthen further the rapport you have been building with your prospect. As the prospect talks about herself, your questions also build on the trust you have created earlier in your presentation. Questioning at this stage of the closing process often puts a prospect in a position where she ends up selling herself.

After you have begun to establish rapport, asked the provocative question, and used the take-away transition technique, you have paved the way for the next step: probing for sales opportunities. The take-away creates a perfect transition for you.

"I'm not certain the logo mats and linen rental package I have in mind will work for your restaurant chain, Jim. Let me get some more information about your locations and present supplier to see if my ideas might be appropriate for your organization."

You have created the perfect opportunity to probe further for more information. You have done it so smoothly and comfortably that your prospect now wants to give you what you need, because he is concerned he might not be able to qualify for the products you have suggested!

1 Ask Open-Ended Questions

To improve your ability to close more sales, you need to learn to use open-ended questions. In communication with prospects, questioning is the edge you have that can make any interview, seminar, or meeting into a two-way discussion or dialogue rather than a one-way sales pitch or monologue. Without conversation between parties, it is impossible to close sales consistently through an interactive process. Once you can influence a prospect to focus on his problems or needs, you usually have a good chance of concluding a transaction if your products or services are the solutions to the need or opportunity you uncover.

The best way to get prospects talking is to ask them open-ended questions. An open-ended question avoids a "yes" or "no" response and usually causes a person to explain or provide you with more information. Look at these examples:

Closed-ended: *"Do you think these phalanges might work for you?"*

Open-ended: *"What are your feelings about how the Teflon-coated phalanges we just discussed might assist your client with his problem?"*

Once you have found an area needing attention, you should ask questions that will help you summarize each point you have made. By consistently asking questions, you can make certain that the prospect understands the concepts and benefits of your products or services before proceeding to the next point.

Open-ended questioning also helps you judge whether your solution is a sound one for a given customer or client and will tell you the progress you are making toward a mutual conclusion. Questions also help a prospect become "yes"-conditioned. The more your prospect agrees with you, the more unreasonable an arbitrary turndown will seem later on when you ask for the sale.

When starting to probe after your take-away transition, try to avoid asking a product- or service-specific question like: "What services are you looking for?" Remember, you do not want to be caught in the product or service discussion trap, as discussed earlier. Instead, use a broader, open-ended question, such as "What kinds of activities are you involved in that require this service?"

If at any time your prospect appears to wonder why you are asking probing questions, simply remind her of her original interest: "We have several ways to help you, but I need to know which of our services (products) will work best for you. That's why I'm asking these questions."

After you have concluded your presentation and you have left the meeting(or your potential customer or client has left your office or store), take a few moments to ask yourself, "What are the things I still don't know about this person or her company?" As you practice this analysis, you will enhance your capacity to obtain the information you need to successfully close sales.

Practice

In the space provided, list as many pieces of information you can think of that you would like to know about one or two of your current prospects, so that you can sell more of your products or services to them:

_____

_____

_____

_____

_____

_____

_____

_____

_____

2 Phrase Questions Carefully

Always allow time for your prospect to provide you with answers or feedback. If you don't, you could risk appearing like an attorney, rapidly firing questions at a witness. A comfortable dialogue should go something like this:

Tom:	*"I thought I'd better review my financial situation before we get too close to the year-end."*
Representative:	*"Good idea, Tom; I hope that implies a good year."*
Tom:	*"It has been. That's why I think we should review the situation and plan ahead."*
Representative:	*"I certainly agree. How does the rest of the year look at this point?"*
Tom:	*"I believe it will continue as strong as ever. Orders are up and the plant is running well above average. I believe we will stay busy well into next year."*
Representative:	*"Since you expect to be even busier, we should schedule our review right away. Tom, if you felt you could review your current situation, get better prepared for the new year, and set the stage for solid long-term planning for the future of your company, would that meet your needs?"*

Use some care in phrasing questions. You want to avoid putting your prospect on the defensive. Remember, you are making business friends, not playing the role of a prosecuting attorney. *Tactfully* phrase each question. Always think about collecting as much information as possible from each person with whom you work. You should want to learn the following information from every prospective client or customer:

➤ If they have purchased your services in the past, what was their experience?

➤ What budget constraints do they have?

➤ Do they have a need for more than one of your services?

➤ Why have they decided to try your company or firm?

When you get this kind of information from your prospects, you will uncover sales opportunities that order-taking staff members never discover.

Practice

Rephrase the following closed-ended questions so they are less apt to make a prospect defensive and more apt to encourage the decision-maker to give you additional information.

Can you afford these services?

_____

_____

_____

Who previously supplied these "U-clamps"?

_____

_____

_____

Do you have a need for any of our other services?

_____

_____

_____

3 Rephrase and Redirect to Maintain Control

To probe successfully for needs, occasionally rephrase your prospect's comments, feed them back in your own words for clarification, then redirect the discussion with another question. For example:

"Let me see, John, you need prompt service with this project because you have limited time available for reviewing the paperwork."

Rephrasing and redirecting techniques will help you keep the conversation on track if it begins to wander.

Whenever you ask a question, give your prospect some time to respond without interrupting. Then, when the prospect pauses, you can rephrase and redirect. Try this kind of redirect:

"Tim, since you have recently reorganized your company, I assume you are looking for a professional who can effectively respond to your current situation. First, tell me about your immediate needs."

Now review the closing process you have learned so far by analyzing the following interview. It picks up right after the prospect has introduced himself and the service professional asks, "Are you still with the clinic on Forest Street, Doctor?"

Doctor: *"No, I left the clinic a couple of years ago and started my own practice. It has been a struggle, but I'm finally beginning to see some light at the end of the tunnel. Just in time, too, since my son will start college in the fall. That's why I'm here—to discuss any additional considerations related to his being away."*

Service Professional: *"That's great; where will he be going?"*

Doctor: *"Yale."*

Service Professional: *"I'll be glad to discuss the changes that should be considered under these circumstances. We have a nice program designed for families with college-bound kids—one especially designed to save you money. Does that sound like it might be interesting to you?"*

What did the service professional do right? He used the title of respect, built a little rapport and picked up on a clue or possible sales opportunity to service the doctor's special circumstances. However, he fell into the product trap, with nowhere to go except to discuss this one special service.

Look at it again, as the situation should have been handled:

Service Professional:	(Makes a mental note about his financial situation). *"Doctor Smoot, that is great news about your son and your practice. What do you think has contributed to your success?"*
Doctor:	*"Well, I have really tried to maintain high standards, while keeping my fees affordable. That's not easy today with medical malpractice rates what they are. But I know I'm doing something right when I compare my progress to that of some of my colleagues who started their practices at the same time."*
Service Professional:	*"Tell me, Doctor, what made you decide to come to us for your special needs?"*
Doctor:	*"Well, Mark, you have worked with me to keep your services affordable, so I thought I'd start with your firm."*
Service Professional:	(Having identified one of his hidden needs, it is time for the provocative question!) *"Doctor Smoot, if you felt you could qualify for a special program designed for college-bound students and discover additional cost-effective methods to prepare for other family members to attend college, would you have time now to talk over these ideas?"*
Doctor:	*"Yes, I'd like that. What are my options relating to programs for my son?"* (The doctor is unintentionally trying to control the discussion by focusing on products.)
Service Professional:	*"There are several ways to handle your son's needs, depending on your situation, but I'm not sure if any of these ideas will be exactly right for you, Doctor. May I ask...?"* (take-away transition)
Doctor:	*"Sure."*
Service Professional:	*"What kinds of programs have you already established for financing your children's education?"* (probing question)

Knowing how to communicate effectively is probably 99.9% of the secret to closing success. The techniques presented here are practical methods that can help you immediately improve your skill level—if you begin now to use them. Trying new ways of communicating requires you to move away from your comfort zones—your normal behaviors. If you are willing to take the risk and keep on trying, you will reap great rewards.

4 Deal with Negatives Head-On

During the probing phase of the selling process, you may stumble upon the fact that your buyer has some negative views about your organization, your products, or your services, which stem from past dealings. In some cases, the views might not be hidden at all because the person calls you directly or comes to your office, demanding that you correct an actual or perceived problem. When these situations arise, it is better not to bury them as unresolved problems or to minimize their impact. Instead, deal with the issue head on.

If you have the advantage of knowing the customer or client and his past negative experience, you are forewarned and forearmed. You can bring up the incident in the discussion at the right time—before the customer does. Get it out on the table so you can move beyond this issue and on to building a better, stronger relationship. You handle it by saying:

"Mark, I know there were some problems in the past with the service that was provided to you, but we have progressed since then and have corrected our operations so that incidents of that kind can be avoided now. I have appreciated your business over the years, and I am prepared to provide you with the assistance you want and deserve. Tell me…" (redirect)

If, on the other hand, you are caught unaware of the customer's or client's previous problem, you can focus your full attention on him by doing the following things:

➤ Listen intently.

➤ Thank him for bringing the matter to your attention.

Show your empathy by saying that you "regret" any inconvenience he might have experienced. Never say you're "sorry." Saying you are sorry indicates guilt, and you or your organization may not be guilty. Also, never use the words "I understand," because you may not understand the situation and using these words could backfire on you.

➤ Ask him for advice on how he would like to see his problem corrected.

➤ Define a plan of action.

➤ Get the customer's (client's) commitment to it.

You can show additional empathy and interest by saying something sincere, such as "I can appreciate how you feel," or "That certainly would be upsetting." Then ask for the details and take notes—even if you know the customer or client is wrong. Ask for his advice because only the customer knows what he expects you to do to make the problem right. Sometimes it is not what you would assume he wants.

If he is still feeling negative even though the incident happened a while ago, it is obvious that someone else did not take the time or care enough about him to "bandage his wounds." Yet, for some positive reason, he has returned, and you now have the opportunity to correct the negative impression. Then you can get on with the business of probing for opportunities and needs to sell your products or services.

Here are some examples of how to turn negatives around and overcome objections.

"I can appreciate how you feel, Sharon."

"I had a similar experience and felt the same way as you, until I realized…."

These are based on a technique referred to as the:

Feel…

Fell…

Realized…

Method

This is another method of redirecting the thoughts of your prospect, customer, or client to a positive frame of mind. Just remember to use phrases like these appropriately and sincerely.

4 Deal with Negatives Head-On (CONTINUED)

Never Make Negative Comments About Your Competition

Let us talk for a moment about how to handle negative comments you hear about your competition. There are three important rules about criticizing the competition: Don't, Don't, and Don't! Here is what you can do:

➤ Ask questions tactfully about what a prospect liked or disliked about a competitor.

➤ Never criticize the competition or agree with a prospect's negative comments about a competitor.

➤ "Appreciate" how a customer or prospect might feel, but refrain from making a comment such as "I don't blame you for feeling that way; I would be upset too."

The best way to compete with other professionals is:

➤ Be aware of what competitors are offering.

➤ Be knowledgeable about how your own products or services compare with theirs.

➤ Know the advantages of working with your company or firm and point them out to your prospect.

5 Use the Most Powerful Principle in Communications

To gain an edge with a prospect, you need to apply the most powerful principle in communications. It is a principle known by various sales trainers and teachers as the "law of psychological reciprocity" and the "power play that never fails." By using this technique, you can gain many true friends. As you use it regularly in selling, you will find that you can gain a great deal of respect and trust from prospects. It is so powerful that it even works on rebellious teenagers. Yet this is a skill that is seldom practiced. What is this powerful communications tool? It is the art of active listening. Really listening!

CLOSING PRINCIPLE 5

People buy from people who listen to them.

Active listening is a valuable asset in the closing process. It is both a verbal and nonverbal technique. Effective two-way communication includes:

➤ Paying sincere compliments

➤ Asking appropriate open-ended questions

➤ Nodding your head in agreement

➤ Paraphrasing a comment

➤ Displaying a genuine and friendly attitude

➤ Maintaining "right-eye" contact

When a prospect or even another staff member is reinforced with these values, he is instinctively compelled from within to give you some value in return.

Therefore, in an interview you should listen more than you talk. By participating (using two-way communication) in the decision-making process, your prospects are more likely to "buy" the conclusion of your presentation—your products or services. In a two-way interview, you can "influence" buyers simply by hearing their problems and then suggesting solutions. The process is easy to apply. You merely ask open-ended questions and really listen to responses.

PART 4

Demonstrations

That Close

The Demonstration Phase of Closing

Often sales and service professionals talk themselves out of a sale when they begin to make their product or service presentations. They either talk too much, demonstrate the wrong features and benefits, or use a pitch that misses the mark altogether.

Demonstrating a product or service so that your presentation assists you in closing is a process and not a problem.

CLOSING PRINCIPLE 6

People justify their buying decisions with their intellect.

Remember, an effective product or service demonstration is rooted in two important closing principles:

Most people *buy* from their emotions.

Then they *justify* their buying decision with their intellect.

Though not all people will follow these two principles in this order when making a buying decision, the vast majority of your prospects will buy emotionally and then try to find ways to justify their decision.

Are you using a "pitch?" A truly persuasive presentation that helps to close your sale is never a hard-sell "pitch" or a "canned demonstration," even though some of the words you use to describe your products and services may be the same each time you discuss them. Using words or sentences that have proven effective and persuasive in past presentations is not the same as giving a sales pitch.

Your presentation should always be based on what you have learned about a prospect's situation and needs, not on what you feel comfortable in selling or on a memorized pitch. You can find out about your prospect's problems, wants, and desires as you ask open-ended questions.

The Demonstration Phase of Closing (CONTINUED)

Pitching products is an inefficient method of sales. Most prospects won't have enough time to listen to all the pitches you need to make just to find the right product or service that meets their need. Many sales and services professionals have over 80 to 100 products or services that could be discussed, making it impossible (from the law of averages) to conduct just the right presentation consistently.

When a demonstration is product-oriented rather than prospect-oriented, most people "tune out" the conversation and start finding ways to end the discussion. As they begin thinking about other things, prospects often miss presentations about products and services that could help them, simply because they are not listening. Yet many sales and service industry professionals still use the pitch approach to selling, then wonder why they are not more effective in closing or in improving their sales ratio.

Find out what will best suit a prospect before you make your presentation, then discuss only those benefits in your demonstration. Using this method, you not only save time, but also have a much better chance of having her hear your presentation. If a prospect cannot or will not hear the benefits your products and services have to offer, there is little chance of completing a sale.

The Five Elements of Closing Demonstrations

A closing demonstration has five basic elements.

1 It focuses on the customer or client benefits that were identified in the in-depth probing phase of the closing process.

2 It gives solid proof of the worth of the benefits you demonstrate.

3 It uses visual aids to enhance the sales process and give prospects a vision of the worth of a product or service being sold.

4 It assesses a prospect's feelings about what he or she has been shown and told.

5 It answers a prospect's objections as if they were questions and views these objections as buying signals.

As with any formula or recipe, if you leave some of the elements out or fail to execute them properly, you may see a reduction in your ability to close.

CASE STUDY: AN OBVIOUS NEED

In a sales presentation to a bank, it became evident to the sales representative that there was a need for the bank's executive vice president to not only find a sales-training firm that could meet his financial institution's training specifications, but also help the executive redeem himself from a training disaster he had presided over the previous year. At one point in the earlier training, the workshop instructor, who had been engaged to train managers (calling officers) at the bank, had been so upset by one of the officer's questions and comments that he threw his marker at the officer. In anger, the instructor told the manager, "If you know so much about this subject, why don't you come up and train the class yourself!" The training session then proceeded to go downhill from there.

On learning about the executive's problems with a competitive training firm, it was obvious that a demonstration of the training modules the sales professional was proposing would have to center around how her training firm would make this senior banking executive look good. Her demonstration would have to convince him that he would receive positive recognition for engaging her company to do his training, rather than focusing on specific benefits of the training modules that the executive was considering.

CASE STUDY ANSWERS: THE WINNING SOLUTION

As illustrated by the case study outlined on the previous page, the representative's demonstration included the following:

- She focused entirely on how good former clients felt using her training organization. At this point, she did not even mention the unique benefits of her calling officer training.

- She included several endorsement letters from other executives satisfied with the benefits they had received from using her training programs. The endorsements contained feedback on how good the participants felt about the quality of instruction. This addressed the executive's underlying fear that he would not be able to recoup from his previous training disaster with his staff.

- She illustrated the specific rewards of her program with visual aids. The salesperson knew she needed to paint a mental picture showing the specific rewards the executive would receive from engaging her services.

- She used trial closings to determine the executive's interest. This helped the salesperson zero in on the concerns he had about her proposed training engagement. One concern was pricing.

- She answered his concern (objection) as if it were nothing more than a question. She talked at length with the executive and told him his participants would receive not only a workbook, but also a text with the training.

- She stressed both the pricing and the personal acclaim he would receive for having purchased the program.

The executive was not only satisfied by the positive reports from his staff members enrolled in the training, but by midafternoon he became so enthusiastic that he called the senior partners of a law firm in his bank building to tell them how great the program was going. He then set up an appointment for the training company's sales representative to meet with the partners of the law firm so that they too could learn how to market and sell their legal services better. As this case study illustrates, sometimes to sell your products or services you may need to focus on something other than the specific features and benefits they have to offer.

Appeal to Your Prospect's Emotions

As you probe for sales opportunities, you should make mental and written notes, if necessary, of your prospect's needs while you listen intently to what she has to say. At the same time, you can begin to analyze which of your organization's wares would best meet the needs that you have uncovered. When it is time for you to present your products (services), you should have already identified which ones are the most appropriate for your prospect. Because of your evaluation, you are now ready to make a presentation that will help you close the sale. At this point, be assertive! Say,

"Based on our discussion, Mary, this is what I think might work for you. First...."

This is the time to think of yourself as an expert. After all, you know much more about your products or services than any of your prospects. However, don't overwhelm them by rattling off all the features of your products (services). Instead, present the benefits of the most appropriate product or service for your prospect, based on what you have learned about her. Remember the differences between "features" and "benefits."

Features are the characteristics about your products (services) that are important to your company, but not necessarily to your prospects, clients, or customers. They are the technical aspects of your products (services) that make them exactly like, or different from, your competitors' offerings. You must not forget that the appeal of a specific product (service) lies in its *benefits*, not its features. Until you translate your service features into specific client benefits, you will rarely make as many sales as you could. Benefits answer this question for a prospect: "What's in it for me?" You can effectively translate service features into benefits by using this helpful phrase

"What this means to you is...."

For example, if you were talking with a prospect about the features of a specific product (service), you might say, "What this means to you is that your middle managers will have long-term access to our senior staff and partners while you have your own account representatives and service team to work through daily challenges."

Three Important Rules

As you demonstrate your products (services), remember these three important rules:

RULE 1 Suggest only those products (services) that meet identified needs.

RULE 2 Continually translate service features into benefits by using the phrase "What this means to you is...."

RULE 3 Avoid discussing in too much detail the specifics of your products (services) until your prospect has agreed to the sale based on the benefits presented in your demonstration. When the prospect says "yes," then disclose all the details of how your product (service) will meet the specific needs of your prospect. If you have compliance issues (bankers, stockbrokers, etc.) that must be discussed, wait until after the sale is made to bring up these topics.

Give Intellectual Proof

It is important that as you appeal to a prospect's emotions in your demonstrations, you are always prepared to give intellectual proof of the benefits that you have outlined. Often a product or service demonstration will consist simply of these intellectual proofs without first appealing to a prospect's emotions. However, once you learn about the need to get in touch with a person's feelings in your demonstration, make certain that you don't swing the pendulum too far and forget to demonstrate the logic behind your emotional appeal.

For example, in the illustration of the banking executive who purchased training based on his need to recoup from an earlier disastrous training session, the primary demonstration appealed to his emotions by telling him how participants felt after training sessions and how the salesperson was able to generate these feelings in individual participants. In this demonstration, she underscored the many years of experience she had in training calling officers. As suggested earlier, she then used endorsement letters as *intellectual proof* of her claims and highlighted specific paragraphs that underpinned the emotional appeal she had made.

Try to obtain endorsement letters (if you are in an industry that allows these tools) from every satisfied customer or client you work with. Endorsement letters not only appeal to a prospect's emotions, but also give prospects the intellectual assurances they need to justify their strong feelings about buying your products (services).

The best method of obtaining an endorsement letter is to ask if you might write one that the executive can put on his or her stationery. This way, you can custom-tailor endorsements that will help you answer objections or reinforce important points in your presentation. Most executives are busy and will appreciate the fact that you have taken some of the work off their hands. If a satisfied customer or client agrees to write a letter for you, make certain that you suggest certain areas for them to cover.

Along with endorsement letters, intellectual proof can consist of:

➤ Charts and graphs

➤ Comparative analysis (weighing the positives against the negatives)

➤ Statistical summaries

➤ Recognition or quality service awards

➤ Consumer ratings and reports

➤ Articles and independent critical evaluations

➤ Vendor endorsements

Any element in your demonstration that primarily appeals to your prospect's logic will help a prospective customer (client) justify a purchase decision based on your emotional appeal.

Product Knowledge

A study was conducted some years ago by a major Wall Street brokerage firm into the investment recommendations of the average stockbroker representing that firm. The information contained in the final report was difficult for the senior executives of the wire house to accept, because they had worked hard to encourage their branches to mount full product-line promotional strategies. Yet the research indicated that most of the firm's stockbrokers had recommended only a few of the thousands of investment products that the brokerage had made available to them. The average registered representative only recommended from five to seven of the firm's approved products, even though management had developed elaborate campaigns and monetary incentives to persuade brokers to offer a wider range of investments.

Give Intellectual Proof (CONTINUED)

This firm's research basically reinforced what psychologists have know for many years—that it is difficult for the human mind to cope effectively with the intricacies of more than seven major concepts at a given time. The stockbrokers were just falling in line with the limitations imposed on them by the way their brain stores and retrieves information. Although their recommendations would change periodically, the average broker would only be comfortable enough with a small number of the firm's products to make a solid presentation. Most of the stockbrokers surveyed concentrated the majority of their promotional efforts only on the two or three investment opportunities that they really understood.

Sales and service professionals in almost every field have the same problem as stockbrokers when representing a multiple line of products or services. The following technique can help you overcome the fear and worry that many of you feel about not having enough "product knowledge" to make an effective demonstration of all the products (services) that you represent.

CASE STUDY: WHEN IT COMES TO PRODUCT KNOWLEDGE—LEARN TO CHEAT!

In a training session at a banking institution, the manager and training staff all agreed that the last role-play of the day was an exceptional performance. After the training was concluded, several of the participants suggested that the customer service representative who made the last presentation deserved some form of special financial recognition for outstanding efforts in learning and presenting the material in such a persuasive manner.

The group had been conducting video role-plays to help customer service representatives make better needs-oriented, cross-sales presentations as they opened new accounts in their respective branches. Most of the participants had not practiced the concepts on the job, so they were not performing the role-plays with a high degree of proficiency. However, when Cindy

CONTINUED

CONTINUED

completed her transaction in front of the camera, her peers as well as the training staff broke into spontaneous applause. In her role-play, Cindy had used every one of the steps she had been taught three weeks earlier in a two-day Cross-Sales Success Strategies workshop that had been custom designed for her financial institution.

In spite of having to perform on camera, in front of her peers, and with a manager in the classroom, Cindy's presentation was almost flawless. This was an exceptional occurrence for this type of workshop, because the bank's employees were just starting to learn cross-sales success techniques.

After the session, the trainers discussed ways to reward Cindy for the work she had done in preparing for her role-play. Cindy suddenly returned to the training center and sheepishly admitted that she had cheated on her exercise. As she left the building, her conscience had worked on her to the point that she decided to return to tell why she had performed so well in her video presentation.

Nobody had noticed Cindy looking down from time to time at the day planner the bank had given her to use in the sales process. Before her role-play, Cindy had made notes outlining the steps in the process she had been taught. She put the notes in her planner and used them to perform the best first-time role-play presentation the trainers had ever witnessed. They were even more impressed with Cindy after her confession. The bank gave her a $100 bonus for her outstanding performance and her creative thinking, even though she admitted to cheating on the exercise.

Give Intellectual Proof (CONTINUED)

Retrieving Information

As you learn presentation skills and effective sales techniques, your brain stores these promotional approaches along with product data, the names of customers, and a million other bits of information in your subconscious mind. However, if these ideas and concepts are not immediately and repeatedly reinforced, it is difficult for most of us to retrieve important information when we really need it. This inability to retrieve important details is most acute when you are under pressure. Your brain seems to automatically stop functioning the minute you find yourself with a disgruntled person or in an intimidating situation. You can overcome this natural and somewhat universal problem by using the methods below.

➤ Compile a book that outlines the basic benefits and intellectual proofs of each product (service) your organization offers.

➤ If your company or firm provides a product book, personally underline pertinent information.

➤ Write personal notes in the margin.

➤ Mark the benefits for easy reference as you make your sales presentations.

➤ Write down the sales techniques or product information you want to remember, then refer to your notes as you make your sales presentation.

➤ Use sales literature to help remember benefits and important proofs as you talk about your products (services).

You can easily make up notes on specific sales techniques, product information, answers to objections, etc., and put them in a notebook, in a day planner, or on file cards. These notes can then be referenced as you execute your product presentation in each transaction. Your prospect will rarely, if ever, notice your use of notes, but as you use them, you will find that your sales presentations will improve dramatically.

By cataloging and indexing your sales literature, or by personally marking a product book to make the benefits and key bits of information stand out, you have created a powerful tool for overcoming the fear of not knowing a product well enough to discuss it effectively. Using references to help you remember a sales technique or proof of the worth of a product (service) is far more professional than failing to make a sale due to a lack of information or stumbling through a transaction, talking off the top of your head, and not being accurate in the information that you present.

Using Visual Aids

People respond well to simple language and vivid mental pictures that are clear and understandable. Listen to the words you and your co-workers use as you interact with prospects, customers, or clients. Then challenge yourself to "keep each demonstration or presentation simple." When you speak, you need to paint word pictures. Mental pictures help you communicate more effectively with your prospects. In sales, the more you can appeal to a person's emotions through word pictures or actual pictures in your demonstration, the greater your chances are of making a sale. Remember that in selling, the saying "A picture is worth a thousand words" is true.

Visual aids can take the form of:

➤ A flip chart

➤ Graphics or illustrations in a printed sales brochure

➤ A legal pad or plain piece of paper on which you illustrate a point by drawing a picture or a chart

Give Intellectual Proof (CONTINUED)

Just going through the main headings of a sales or capabilities brochure with a prospect and pointing out selected concepts can have a tremendous impact on your sales success.

Using visual aids can help you as much as they help your prospect. Sales aids, such as flip charts, brochures, and product books, can be used as a prompt to include important details during your presentation. These aids also help prospective customers or clients visualize each of the personal benefits your products (services) have to offer.

To reinforce the important features and benefits of a product (service) with your prospect, briefly review concepts presented in a brochure and discuss the advantages of the features. Use a yellow marker or red pen to highlight or underline the benefits. Many times, prospects will need to think over the points you have made or discuss them with their boss, board, staff, or family members. If you give them a highlighted brochure to take with them (or send it as a softener at a later time), these highlighted headings and passages will stand out on the page and help reinforce the main selling points you have made in your demonstration.

If you are presenting the benefits of a specific product (service), use a notepad or paper as a sales tool. In bold letters, list the following as you discuss each point in your demonstration:

Product (Service) Heading:

➤ Benefit One

➤ Benefit Two

➤ Benefit Three

With your product knowledge, you should know how to explain the personal benefits of each feature in detail. Your prospect's eyes will focus on the written words as you talk in word pictures, and an image about each personal benefit will be imprinted in your prospect's mind. As with any sales technique, the effective use of flip charts or yellow-pad illustrations takes practice, and you should spend some time working with these tools to become familiar with their formats and the script you will use.

Ask Trial Closing Questions

Trial closing is a demonstration skill worth learning. Often you will demonstrate a feature of a product (service), but fail to bring the benefit into focus for your prospects. As suggested earlier, by simply remembering to say, "What this means to you is…," you can move the product (service) features into customer (client) benefits. Then by asking, "Does this make sense to you?" or, "Will this meet your needs?" or, "Will this solve your problem?" you can determine if the prospect really understands how your product (service) will work for him. This procedure is called a "trial closing." When you use trial closings throughout your presentation, your final closing should be much easier.

Here are some examples:

"Does this package of services make sense to you?"

"What do you think about the benefits of these programs?"

"How does this approach sound to you?"

"Do you feel this product will meet your needs?"

"Other than yourself, is anyone else in the company leadership involved in the final decision-making process?"

"What other information do you need before making a decision?"

Ralph Waldo Emerson said, "The highest price you can pay for a thing is to ask." If we apply this quotation to the closing process, it means that many sales and service professionals feel that asking for the business is the most difficult aspect of closing a sale. Often this is due to their fear of rejection or fear of looking foolish. In an effective sales presentation, as you move from your demonstration phase to asking for the business (closing), you need to ask a few trial closing questions along the way to eliminate the fear of asking for a sale and make tying down the sale easier. Trial closing questions ask for opinions—for prospect feedback.

Practice

Create a dialogue between you and your prospect, focusing on trial closing questions.

_____

_____

_____

_____

_____

_____

_____

_____

Summarize the features and benefits of the products (services) you have discussed before you ask a trial closing question. The summary should be short and to the point, outlining the facts and emphasizing each benefit. Next, ask a trial closing question. As you respond to any concerns your prospect might have, present your solutions by reemphasizing the benefits of your product or service. Then ask for the sale.

It works like this:

"Jerry, you indicated that you have needed professional advice and assistance in the marketing area of your business for quite some time. The package of services we discussed has helped many of our clients eliminate this problem by giving them peace of mind that these issues are being handled professionally and in a timely fashion. As we discussed, we have a special program right now that would allow you to try out our sales training on a trial basis at no cost if you are not completely satisfied with our results. (Summary)

How does this program sound to you? (Trial Closing Question) [Wait for a response; if it is positive, continue.]

May I set an appointment with you for our initial fact finder for the first of next week?" (Close)

Answer Objections as Questions, Not as a Roadblock to Your Sale!

As your prospect responds to your trial closing questions, you must listen carefully to his response to determine how best to proceed. For example, a prospect might say:

"I like the fact that I can buy these replacement filters in smaller quantities, but I feel the cost of the just-in-time plan is a bit excessive."

The prospect is not saying that he does not want to buy from you; he is merely making you aware that he has some concerns. When a prospect raises an objection, he is usually not saying "no" to your sale, he is simply asking for clarification or for an assurance that his purchase is a wise decision.

Think of objections as:

> ➤ Questions a prospect has as she ponders your demonstration

> ➤ Opportunities to make not just one sale, but many sales

> ➤ Stepping stones to reach a desired sales objective

> ➤ Buying signals (because your prospect wants to be reassured that she is on the right track)

You have heard the phrase "the best defense is a good offense." It applies not only in sports but in closing a sale, as well. The best way to deal with objections is to be prepared for them. If you were asked to list the most common objection that prospects have to each of your products (services), could you do it? You probably could compile such a list. When you are aware of common objections, you can prepare yourself for overcoming them. You should gather information that supports your defense—statistics, testimonials, other opinions, etc—so you are prepared to discuss the subject if needed.

Every prospect you encounter needs to be valued and understood. If an objection is raised during your demonstration or anytime in the process, view it as a question and proceed to give your prospect the information he needs in a manner that shows you value his concerns.

OVERCOMING OBJECTIONS

In the space provided, indicate some of the frequent objections you hear about your products (services). Then describe a response you could use to overcome the objection.

PRODUCT 1: _____

Objections:

_____

_____

_____

Responses:

_____

_____

_____

PRODUCT 2: _____

Objections:

_____

_____

_____

Responses:

_____

_____

_____

Abraham Lincoln was an outstanding lawyer who rarely lost a case. His biographers suggest that the reason may have stemmed from his unwillingness to argue with or attack an opponent. They note, in fact, that Lincoln was most often found pointing out the shrewdness of his opponents' arguments. Next, he would suggest that there were "other considerations" to be kept in mind, and he then developed his case around those other considerations. You can learn a lesson from Lincoln's treatment of people. Rather than viewing a prospect's objection as a challenge or a point of argument, value it as a legitimate concern to be acknowledged, evaluated, and overcome by looking at other considerations.

A most effective technique for pointing out to clients the "other considerations" is one you have already learned:

"I appreciate how you feel, Jim. Some of my other clients felt the same way until they realized…."

You empathize with your prospect when you listen with interest to what he says, respond with care, and accept his objections as opinions or concerns that have value. When you empathize, you put into action the law of "psychological reciprocity." Sincerely showing your prospects and clients that you value their feelings and ideas causes them instinctively to value you in return.

Beginning the Close

As sales and services professionals are observed in actual sales situations in the field with potential customers (clients), instead of boldly asking their prospect for the sale, many sellers wait for the decision-maker to say, "That sounds great. I would love to work with you. How do we get started?" or, "The products you have described look like the best option. I'll take them." Using the systematic closing process outlined in this manual, often a prospect will ask how she can get started or how she can buy the products offered. However, when a prospect fails to indicate that she would like to begin using the products (services) presented, many professionals assume that the prospect has no interest and that there is no chance of making a sale. If you wait for a prospect to initiate the action that will close your transaction, you could risk losing the sale altogether.

An interesting phenomenon frequently occurs when a prospective customer (client) faces a buying decision. A "barrier of fear" arises that must be neutralized before the sale can be completed. Fear can keep a prospect from buying even when she is convinced the products (services) you have demonstrated will help her and her company perform better. Fear of making bad decisions, what other people will think, or making changes can become a formidable obstacle to closing, unless you realize that the "fear barrier" is a natural part of the closing process.

An effective method for alleviating a prospect's fear is to give the decision-maker permission to tell you "no." Just say,

"Sara, I want your business, but if what I have proposed won't work for you, it would be a mistake to proceed, so please feel free to tell me no. This way I won't keep trying to persuade you to do something that's not right and waste both of our time in the process."

Giving a decision-maker permission to tell you "no" also helps to keep you from building up long list of prospects who have told you they have to "think over" your proposal and will get back to you. "I've got to think it over…" is a stall that is used in place of the words "No, thank you!" because it is difficult for most buyers to come right out and tell you "no."

Reinforcing the benefits of your products or services and reemphasizing value can also alleviate the barrier of fear. It is done like this:

"What this means to you, Michelle, is that you will have better peace of mind knowing this area has been taken care of...etc."

When you understand what objections are, why they occur, and how you can best react to them, you raise the level of your communication skills and increase your overall closing effectiveness.

Prospects usually raise objections due to one of the following three reasons:

1. You failed to follow the closing steps outlined here and have reverted to an order-taking mode of selling.

2. If you have executed the closing process effectively, you are likely dealing with someone who cannot make a decision or is not the decision-maker.

3. There is a hidden objection that has not come to the surface as you describe the prospect's various options.

In all three cases, it is important that you isolate your prospect's objections so that you can determine which of the three areas listed above are at the root of your problem.

In order to isolate an objection, you need to ask a question something like this:

"If it weren't for this problem, Molly, would you purchase these disks today?"

or,

"Sam, are there any other things that are troubling you about our discussion, or is this the only area concerning you at this time?"

Beginning the Close (CONTINUED)

By asking a question that isolates a buyer's objection, you can determine whether or not your prospect's concern is a legitimate problem you failed to uncover and discuss in your presentation. The objection may also be a clumsy attempt by your customer to stop the sales process from moving forward, because he either doesn't like making decisions or is not the decision-maker. Often there are hidden objections that do not come out during your presentation because the individual feels uneasy about discussing the situation. By isolating an objection, you should be able to recognize the problem and take the appropriate action to overcome it.

If your prospect's objection is legitimate, and you isolate it to find that there are only one or two other issues that might keep him from completing the transaction, you simply have to show him how your products (services) can meet needs and overcome fears or concerns. You can then proceed with the closing of the transaction. If there are multiple objections, especially after you have conducted an effective presentation, you know that there must be a hidden objection. In this case, your prospect is likely not going to purchase due to some hidden motive.

Often, multiple objections at this stage are frivolous and not worth considering. This is a clue to let you know that your buyer is not being honest with you about his intentions. When you run into this problem, there is very little you can say to overcome a hidden objection, especially if your prospect will not reveal it to you. If the hidden objection is the fact that someone else will have to make the decision, try asking:

"Is there anyone else who needs to discuss these accounts before we get started on the paperwork?"

or,

"Along with you, is there anyone else who will be involved in this decision?"

The genuine prospect (a person with money and authority to make and back up his buying decision) who is reluctant to buy after seeing your presentation and after favorably answering your trial closing questions may have real reasons for hesitancy. Perhaps you have not executed the steps in the selling (closing) process outlined in this guide accurately, and questions remain unanswered or concerns have not yet been fully discussed. In a nonthreatening manner, try a probing question such as:

"What concerns do you still have, Don, that prevent you from taking advantage of our services today?"

or,

"We have discussed at length how (specific services) will benefit you, Gina; perhaps I can answer the questions you still have regarding them?"

At no time should you make your prospect feel uncomfortable or pressured. However, you owe it to yourself and your organization to make a second effort to learn what a person's hidden concerns really are. Also, by giving your prospect permission to tell you "no" at this stage of your sale, you can often get her to open up to you and tell you exactly how she feels or what she is thinking.

If your second try proves unproductive and the prospect says, "I really don't have any concerns; I just want to rethink all this information and get back to you with my decision," you must allow her to do so. However, when a prospect needs to think over" or "talk over" your proposal with someone else, try asking:

"Can I interpret this as a definite sign of interest on your part?"

Beginning the Close (CONTINUED)

The answer to this question will let you know if your prospect is just stalling and you are wasting your time, or if you should pursue this transaction further. After asking where you stand and giving a potential customer (client) permission to tell you "no," if you feel you have a legitimate opportunity to make a sale, you need to close on a future appointment to close the sale. When applying this rule, you would say something like this to your prospect:

"I appreciate your desire to carefully analyze this purchase. Let's set up an appointment for next week after you've had time to think this through. Would Tuesday or Wednesday be better for you?"

Then you should write down the appointment in front of your prospect and even put it on the back of your business card and hand it to him as a reminder of the meeting time.

Sometimes you can avoid the occurrence of this situation altogether by qualifying the prospect in a provocative question. For example:

"Beth, if you felt… **(benefits)** *…, would you purchase this* **(product or package)** *today?"*

As you practice the techniques you have studied, you will learn what works with certain types of people and you will become more skilled at all aspects of closing. You need to be conscious of how each of the steps outlined here can help you in achieving your objective of tying off a sale, while you repeatedly practice each technique you have been given.

Never accept rejections at face value. For example, when your prospect says, "I want to think it over," it is often just a polite way of telling you "No!" You may think it is a stall and that all you need to do is to go along with your prospect, then he will come back in a short period and buy those products (services) you have recommended. The fact is, "I've got to think it over" is a final statement and rarely will your prospect return with a positive answer.

However, there are ways to help you overcome this type of objection:

1. Listen without interrupting.

2. Agree that it is a big decision.

3. Question what it is that the person wants to think over by asking:

   "Is it our rates or pricing?"

   "Is it the integrity of our company or firm?"

   "Is it me?"

4. Isolate the objection, then ask, *"If it weren't for this, would you open these accounts today?"*

As suggested earlier, demonstrations that help you close are rooted firmly in presenting those products (services) that fill a need or overcome problems that you learn about through in-depth questioning. This means that your demonstration is focused and custom-tailored to help each prospect achieve specific goals or objectives. This will work better than a canned pitch that has little or no meaning for your prospect.

By providing companies or individuals with the exact products (services) that meet their needs, you are also building mutually profitable, long-term customer (client) relationships.

Closing Is a

Process

Finalizing Your Sale

The final step in the closing process is tying down your sale and taking action. This means that both the sales or service professional and the prospect should be able to satisfy their personal needs. If each of the preceding steps outlined in this guide is executed properly, then closing can be the easiest activity in the entire procedure.

Closing should also set the stage for future business. You need to remember that the sale does not end when your interview concludes or even when a prospect says, "Not this time." Real selling means persistence. When a prospect says, "Not now," you need to follow up repeatedly until the prospect says, "Yes" or "Go away." Sometimes in sales, the timing is not right for a customer (client) to decide. However, if a rapport has been developed between you and your prospect, sales can eventually be made as long as you stay in touch with the prospect and keep trying for a "Yes." Successful professionals are persistent.

CLOSING PRINCIPLE 7

People buy from professionals who ask for their business.

Finalizing Your Sale (CONTINUED)

Be Human

Gerhard Gschwandtner, publisher of *Personal Selling Power*, has stated, "Salespeople must remember to be human beings. The problem with a lot of salespeople is they've been trained to become sales automatons—to sell a standardized product with a standardized approach that uses a routine for questioning and formulas for closing." Gschwandtner is talking about salespeople—those who use memorized closing tactics to achieve their sales goals. By stating that salespeople need to be "human beings," he was suggesting that today's sales representatives need to use selling and closing techniques that concentrate on helping consumers define their needs and then finding ways to meet those needs. This approach also appears to be more accepted by consumers today, since most prospects see through canned sales pitches and manipulative techniques that many sales representatives pass off as closing skills.

The excessive use of manipulative closing techniques and formulas stems from a lack of understanding about selling at the management or leadership level within many firms or businesses. Often sales managers, managing partners, business development officers, or business owners place an inordinate amount of pressure on their sales or service industry professionals to "close more sales." These leaders view closing as the only valid activity in the sales process worth learning. In those few organizations that teach selling, often instruction on closing techniques and product knowledge are passed off as an effective sales training curriculum. These people feel that low sales performance is caused by a lack of closing skills. Once a representative or accountant, engineer, optician, etc., learns a few closing tactics, managers think that they will see dramatic increases in sales, only to learn that this approach seldom works to improve business.

Some authors and trainers rank the closing step in the sales process second only to "qualifying" or probing for needs. Yet closing relies so heavily on building a level of trust, learning about needs, and then showing how a prospect's needs can be met that it should rank as last in the closing process outlined in this manual. Prospective customers (clients) see buying as a natural outgrowth of a professional presentation, not the result of specific, high-pressure closing skills.

What <u>Not</u> to Do

Here are some examples of high-pressure closing techniques I found in recently published training manuals:

Pity Close: *"Frankly, my job is on the line here, Cal. If I don't bring in this sale today, I won't have a job tomorrow. Can't you see your way clear to give me this order?"*

Minor Point Close: *"Your boss wouldn't care about such a small purchase, would he?"*

Intimidation Close: *"You do want the unit that makes your spouse happy, don't you?"*

Loaded "Yes" Close: *"Doesn't your family deserve a better model?"*

Guilt Close: *"I'm certain your executive committee is in favor of this concept. Wouldn't it be a good idea to work in accordance with their feelings?"*

Guilt Close: *"I've been working with you for more than a year now. How could you turn your back on such a positive working relationship?"*

Even if these manipulative techniques eventually produce a sale, this aggressive approach will create a negative feeling in most consumers and reduce a salesperson's chance of successfully closing—or of closing any sales in the future.

If you truly are focused on your prospect, her needs, and your ability to fill those needs, then the close should be the natural conclusion to this well-executed process.

Don't use high-pressure closing techniques.

You'll lose more business than you'll get.

Recognizing Buying Signals

Much has been written and said about the "right moment to close." However, in most closing situations there is more than one time when a sale can be concluded. Often a sales representative or service professional may bring the prospect to a buying decision and not even know it. In this case, the prospect may lose interest while the sales or service professional continues to talk. However, in the average sale, there usually is a point when you can detect a rising interest on the part of your prospect. Sometimes a prospective buyer will give off involuntary closing signals that let you know it is time to close without going into more detail. Here are some examples.

Inquiry indicator: When a prospect inquires about the price or terms of your sale, this is an indication of real interest and you can assume she is sold. At this point, stop your demonstration and ask for the sale.

Nonverbal indicator: Watch for nonverbal interest signals. A prospect's attitude and body language can betray interest and set the stage for closing a sale. A decision-maker who leans forward or moves closer to you during your demonstration is often giving off a buying signal. Watch to see if your prospective buyer relaxes by lowering her shoulders and untightening her hands as she accepts your solution. Also, watch to see if the muscles at the corners of her mouth and eyes become relaxed.

These signals often indicate a change in attitude. Never close on just one indicator; wait until you have a group of them. However, the best way to know if a person is ready to buy is simply to ask a trial closing question or two. This should give you the information you need to know how to continue with the process.

A sale really doesn't begin until the prospect says, "No." Often sales and service professionals view the word "no" as a final decision, not realizing that it is human nature to put up a little bit of resistance in a sales situation. Objections are often buying signals. When sellers accept the word "no" at face value, they often miss an opportunity to close sales and solidify strong customer (client) relationships because they believe they will alienate the prospect and lose the sale altogether if they continue to assert themselves.

Research shows that most salespeople, when trying to obtain an appointment, will accept the first "no" as a final decision. However, sales representatives who have been trained to ask a second and third time for a meeting see their appointment closing rate go up significantly as they give the prospect additional benefits and ask a second or third time for an appointment. By asking for an appointment or a buying decision only one time, a representative will close approximately 10% to 30%, depending on the industry. By finding a way to ask a second time (after having been told "no"), closings averaged between 30% to 50%. For those who will ask a third time, after having been told "no" twice, the average closing rate soars to over 60%.

When a prospect objects to your demonstration, this is one of the best closing signals she can give you. When a prospect has an objection, often she is merely saying, "I can't see how your offer meets my needs." She is just asking for clarification rather than trying to shut off further discussion. In addition, asking for clarification is usually a strong buying signal. As the research outlined above indicates, we should never accept an objection (even the word "no") at face value.

Create a Sense of Urgency

Once a prospect's needs are identified and your approach to filling those needs has been explained, one of the best ways to create a sense of urgency and bring a sale to a close is by asking this question:

"Where do we go from here?"

This question requires a decision from a prospect but is nonthreatening. People don't like to be "sold." They like having options and making choices. An effective approach when asking a prospect to buy is to give her several choices. For example:

"Would you prefer our monthly retainer approach, Nancy, or would you rather work on a project-by-project basis?"

Another example is:

"Which of these two models do you feel will best help you meet the needs of your staff, Susan?"

When you ask prospects to choose, you are asking them to make a buying decision, but without the unnatural pressure that accompanies the closing tactics mentioned earlier.

No matter which approach you use to bring a prospect to a buying decision, you must ask a question that will call for a decisionmaker. Once asked, it is time for you to be quiet and wait for an answer. Silence is an important tool in the closing process, but it sometimes makes many sales professionals uncomfortable.

Many people feel compelled to fill in a gap in conversation. As a result, if you are silently waiting, often your prospect will step in to fill the void. Many contracts or transactions are lost each day simply because a professional fails to stop talking long enough to get a positive response from a prospect. A selling professional usually keeps talking because she is uncomfortable asking for the business for fear of seeming overly pushy or aggressive. When you have tactfully followed the steps to closing success outlined in this manual, you should not fear appearing pushy or aggressive. It would actually seem strange to a decision-maker if you completed all the steps and then failed to ask for the business. Therefore, ask your closing question and then remain silent. The first person to speak must be your prospect.

The closing question is used like any other question: You close because you want to know what your prospect is thinking. You must know your prospect's thoughts so you know exactly how to respond to him or what action to take. It is simply a logical part of good communication. That is what closing is all about—knowing how to communicate effectively with people so they will share with you their thoughts and feelings and allow you to help them meet their needs.

Just Ask!

The closing process encourages your prospect to do most of the talking so that you can obtain all the information you need to close the sale. The process also helps eliminate uncertainties or resistance long before they enter your prospect's mind. Let's briefly review the steps one last time.

STEP ONE: Build Rapport

The first step in the closing process consists of building rapport with your prospect, customer, or client. By building rapport, a sales representative or service professional establishes a level of trust that eliminates the prospect's need to resist sales simply because no relationship exists with the seller.

STEP TWO: Capture Attention with Personal Questions

The second step in the closing process requires you to capture the attention of your prospect to help her focus on a series of products (services) that might be beneficial. Use a provocative question to set the stage for in-depth probing. This provocative question can be followed by a "take-away transition." The transition will eliminate any objections a prospect might have to your further probing.

When you use a provocative question, remember to use the words "If you felt…" to begin the question so that you can tap into your prospect's feelings. People buy from their emotions and then justify the decision with their intellect.

STEP THREE: Ask In-Depth Open-Ended Questions

In Step Three of the closing process, you have been taught to ask open-ended questions (questions that require more than a "yes" or "no" answer) to find out exactly where your prospect is coming from. Once you know precisely what his needs and problems are, it is easy to conduct a successful product presentation based strictly on his specific situation.

STEP FOUR: Use Demonstrations That Close

Make certain that your product presentation concentrates on customer benefits and only on those benefits that meet the needs you have discovered in Step Three.

STEP FIVE: Meet Objections Head-On

In order to eliminate most objections and set the stage for closing, make certain that you understand the first four steps in the closing process outlined here. By practicing the steps and focusing on your prospect's needs, you will rarely encounter serious objections as you ask for a sale. Asking trialclosing questions also helps eliminate the problems encountered by those professionals who try to close without first checking on their prospect's feelings.

Should you encounter an objection, always remember to isolate it. Also remember that 95% of the time the words "I need to think this over" are a polite way of telling you "no." Isolate this objection as well to find out exactly where you stand with a buyer. Many objections are great buying signals. Treat them as if they are merely questions, rather than roadblocks to your close. Each time you successfully answer a buyer's question, you are one step closer to finalizing your sale.

STEP SIX: Ask for the Sale!

By using the steps above, instead of a traditional pitch (tellin'/sellin') approach, often your prospective customer or client will ask you, "How do we get started?" Closing the sale (asking for the business or getting a client to take action) is a difficult activity for most professionals in all industries and professions because they simply fail at communicating effectively. In this book, I could have taught you over 50 ways to close a sale; instead, I've chosen to show you that closing is part of an overall effective communications process and not just the use of hard-sell closing levers or techniques.

Summary

Closing a sale is an art and a science. Since prospective customers or clients generally do not like making decisions, closing a sale should be the natural conclusion to a well-executed presentation. At the beginning of this book it was suggested that if you can show your prospect that he is better off with your products or services than without them, then the sale is yours. When a sales presentation is made properly using the six steps outlined here, it should result in new business for your firm. In fact, prospects expect to be asked to use your services or buy your products at the conclusion of your sales presentation. At that point, there really is no need to use special closing techniques. You simply need to ask for their business. Just ask! That is all there really is to closing.

Additional Reading

Alessandra, Tony, Ph.D., Phil Wexler, and Rick Barrera. *Non-Manipulative Selling*. New York: Simon & Schuster, 1992.

Beckwith, Harry. *Selling the Invisible*. New York: Warner Books, 1997.

Beemer, C. Britt, with Robert L. Shook. *Predatory Marketing*. New York: William Morrow, 1997.

Buskirk, Richard H. *Selling Principles and Practices*. New York: McGraw Hill, 1982.

Cialdini, Robert B., Ph.D. *Influence the Psychology of Persuasion*. New York: William Morrow and Company, Inc., 1993.

Clemmer, Jim. *Pathways to Performance*. Rocklin, CA: Prima Publishing, 1995.

Gitomer, Jeffrey H. *The Sales Bible*. New York: William Morrow and Company, Inc., 1994.

Johnson, Spencer. *Who Moved My Cheese?* New York: G. P. Putnam's Sons, 1998.

Malloy, John T. *John T. Malloy's New Dress for Success*. New York: Warner Books, 1987.

Malloy, John T. *Women's Dress for Success Handbook*. New York: Warner Books, 1987.

Morgan, Rebecca L. *Professional Selling: Practical Secrets for Successful Sales*. Menlo Park, CA: Crisp Publications, Inc., 1988.

Reichheld, Frederick F. *The Loyalty Effect*. Boston: Bain and Company, Inc., 1996.

Reilly, Tom. *Value-Added Selling Techniques*. New York: Congdon and Weed, Inc., 1987.

Weylman, Richard C. *Opening Closed Doors Reaching Hard-to-Reach People*. New York: Irwin Professional Publishing, 1994.

NOTES

NOTES

NOTES

NOTES

NOTES

NOTES

NOTES

Now Available From

Books•Videos•CD-ROMs•Computer-Based Training Products

Subject Areas Include:

Management
Human Resources
Communication Skills
Personal Development
Marketing/Sales
Organizational Development
Customer Service/Quality
Computer Skills
Small Business and Entrepreneurship
Adult Literacy and Learning
Life Planning and Retirement

VERK

CRISP WORLDWIDE DISTRIBUTION

English language books are distributed worldwide. Major international distributors include:

ASIA/PACIFIC

Australia/New Zealand: In Learning, PO Box 1051, Springwood QLD, Brisbane, Australia 4127   Tel: 61-7-3-841-2286, Facsimile: 61-7-3-841-1580
ATTN: Messrs. Richard/Robert Gordon

Malaysia, Philippines, Singapore: Epsys Pte Ltd., 540 Sims Ave #04-01, Sims Avenue Centre, 387603, Singapore   Tel: 65-747-1964, Facsimile: 65-747-0162 ATTN: Mr. Jack Chin

Hong Kong/Mainland China: Crisp Learning Solutions, 18/F Honest Motors Building 9-11 Leighton Rd., Causeway Bay, Hong Kong   Tel: 852-2915-7119, Facsimile: 852-2865-2815 ATTN: Ms. Grace Lee

Japan: Phoenix Associates, Believe Mita Bldg., 8th Floor 3-43-16 Shiba, Minato-ku, Tokyo 105-0014, Japan   Tel: 81-3-5427-6231, Facsimile: 81-3-5427-6232
ATTN: Mr. Peter Owans

CANADA

Crisp Learning Canada, 60 Briarwood Avenue, Mississauga, ON L5G 3N6 Canada
Tel: 905-274-5678, Facsimile: 905-278-2801
ATTN: Mr. Steve Connolly

EUROPEAN UNION

England: Flex Learning Media, Ltd., 9-15 Hitchin Street,
Baldock, Hertfordshire, SG7 6AL, England
Tel: 44-1-46-289-6000, Facsimile: 44-1-46-289-2417   ATTN: Mr. David Willetts

INDIA

Multi-Media HRD, Pvt. Ltd., National House, Floor 1
6 Tulloch Road, Appolo Bunder, Bombay, India 400-039
Tel: 91-22-204-2281, Facsimile: 91-22-283-6478
ATTN: Messrs. Ajay Aggarwal/ C.L. Aggarwal

SOUTH AMERICA

Mexico: Grupo Editorial Iberoamerica, Nebraska 199, Col. Napoles, 03810 Mexico, D.F.
Tel: 525-523-0994, Facsimile: 525-543-1173   ATTN: Señor Nicholas Grepe

SOUTH AFRICA

Bookstores: Alternative Books, PO Box 1345, Ferndale 2160, South Africa
Tel: 27-11-792-7730, Facsimile: 27-11-792-7787   ATTN: Mr. Vernon de Haas

Corporate: Learning Resources, P.O. Box 2806, Parklands, Johannesburg 2121, South Africa, Tel: 27-21-531-2923, Facsimile: 27-21-531-2944 ATTN: Mr. Ricky Robinson

MIDDLE EAST

Edutech Middle East, L.L.C., PO Box 52334, Dubai U.A.E.
Tel: 971-4-359-1222, Facsimile: 971-4-359-6500   ATTN: Mr. A.S.F. Karim